LEROY COLLINS LEON COUNTY PUBLIC LIBRARY

WITHDRAW

3 1260 01027 9225

D0145864

THE ROUTLEDGE
HISTORICAL ATLAS
OF THE
AMERICAN SOUTH

THE ROUTLEDGE
HISTORICAL ATLAS
OF THE
AMERICAN SOUTH

ANDREW K. FRANK

MARK C. CARNES, SERIES EDITOR

ROUTLEDGE

NEW YORK AND LONDON

Published in 1999 by
Routledge
29 West 35th Street
New York, NY 10001

Published in Great Britain in 1999 by
Routledge
11 New Fetter Lane
London EC4P 4EE

Text copyright © 1999 by Andrew K. Frank
Maps and design © 1999 by Arcadia Editions Ltd

Printed in the United Kingdom on acid-free paper.

All rights reserved. No part of this book may be reprinted or reproduced or utilized in any form or by any electronic, mechanical, or other means, now known or hereafter invented, including photocopying and recording or in any information storage or retrieval system, without permission in writing from the publishers.

Routledge, Inc. respects international copyright laws. Any omissions or over-sights in the acknowledgments section of this volume are purely unintentional.

10 9 8 7 6 5 4 3 2 1

Library of Congress Cataloging-in-Publication Data

Frank, Andrew, 1970–
    The Routledge historical atlas of the American South / Andrew Frank.
        p. cm. — (Routledge atlases of American history)
    Includes index.
        ISBN 0-415-92135-X (cloth : alk. paper). — ISBN 0-415-92141-4 (pbk : alk. paper)
        1. Southern States—History—Civil War, 1861–1865—Maps. 2. Southern States—History—1865–1877—Maps. 3. Southern States—Social conditions—1865–1945—Maps. 4. Southern States—Economic conditions—Maps. I. Titles. II. Title: Historical atlas of the American South. III. Series.
    G1281.S5 F7 1999 <G&M>
    912.75—DC21
                                                                99–25582
                                                                    CIP
                                                                  MAPS

912.75 Fra
1027 9225 07/31/01   BLP
Frank, Andrew, 1970-

The Routledge historical
atlas of the American
                      KG

LeRoy Collins
Leon County Public Library
200 W. Park Avenue
Tallahassee, FL 32301

Contents

Foreword

When Routledge invited me to serve as general editor of this series, the first title I proposed became this volume. To note that the South warranted special consideration was no act of genius. The South has always been this nation's most distinctive region, and interest in regional history has grown rapidly within the past decade, much of it focused on the South. Scholars have devised specialized courses and academic programs on Southern history, and the subject has stimulated a host of scholarly monographs along with reference works ranging from encyclopedias and biographical collections to guidebooks on language and folkways.

My own awareness of this commonplace was hammered home while I was working on *Mapping America's Past* (1996), a historical atlas of the entire nation. A historical atlas conveys information visually, and I soon learned that the eye is attracted to contrast. What my eye was unavoidably drawn to, in so many national maps, was the South.

This came as little surprise in the maps on presidential politics: the political crisis of the antebellum era culminated in a Civil War whose regional dimension was explicit. The diffusion of cotton cultivation was a consequence of Eli Whitney's invention of the cotton gin in 1793, and of the growing demand for cotton among British and American textile manufacturers. But geography and climate conspired to ensure that the cotton kingdom would be a southern realm. Short-strand cotton flourished in the rich prairies of central Alabama and Mississippi, in the drier upland regions of the South, and especially along the alluvial deposits of the numerous rivers that flowed from the Appalachians into the Gulf of Mexico. Cotton cultivation-and the proliferation of slavery in the regions where it was cultivated-was the signal political fact of the antebellum South. During the century after the Civil War and Reconstruction, unresolved issues of race permeated Southern politics in ways that had no analogue in the rest of the nation.

But I saw that the differences between the South and elsewhere were pronounced in many topics far removed from issues of slavery and race. Southern voters were far more likely to favor imperialism in the 1890s and isolationism during the 1930s, to oppose woman's suffrage in the 1910s and the equal rights amendment for women in the 1970s. In demographic terms, the seventeenth-century South was disproportionately male; and white women in the nineteenth-century South had far more children than white women elsewhere. During the early decades of the twentieth century, literacy rates in the South were lower, as were per capital expenditures on public education. Throughout the past three centuries, religious affiliation has been higher in the South than elsewhere. These and many other differences confirmed the distinctiveness of the South as a region, and its salience for further study.

Andrew K. Frank illuminates these and other singular aspects of Southern society and culture. But even as this volume provides justification for thinking about the South as a region unto itself, it also shows that the South in fact consists of many shifting social and cultural sub-regions. The South has been and still remains a changing kaleidoscope of peoples, economic and political systems, and cultures.

Much is made of this nation's diversity; the same is true, as Frank ably shows, of its most distinctive region.

Mark C. Carnes
Barnard College, Columbia University

Introduction

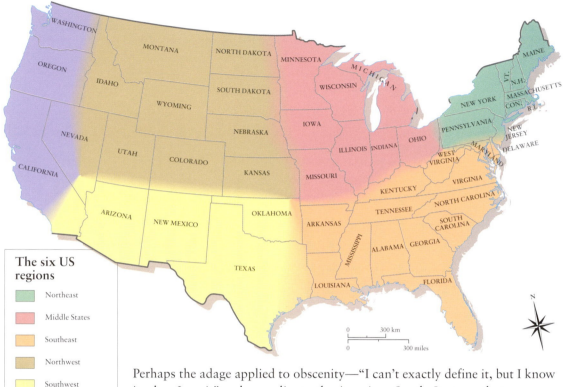

The six US regions

- Northeast
- Middle States
- Southeast
- Northwest
- Southwest
- Far West

Perhaps the adage applied to obscenity—"I can't exactly define it, but I know it when I see it"—also applies to the American South. It seems that everyone recognizes the region's existence, but few can coherently define it. At times it has been a nation, a region within a nation, a relatively cohesive culture, and an area of cultural interaction. It has existed alongside, and sometimes in contrast to, New England, the North, the Union, the West, and even the United States. Parts of it were once Spanish, French, English, Native-American, and English territories. Over time, the American South has changed in meaning, geography, and culture. However, throughout its history the South has been, in the words of historian C. Vann Woodward, "American a long time before it was Southern in any self-conscious or distinctive way. It remains more American by far than anything else, and has all along."

The ambiguous and historical nature of the American South should not deter us from trying to define it. This volume, in large part, is an attempt to offer a historical definition. As the label "American South" implies, it is impossible to define the South without attaching it to a particular place—the southeastern corner of the United States. Yet geography defines as well as divides the region. Several subregions and distinct terrains exist within the American South. There is an Upper South, Lower South, Chesapeake, old Southwest, and Gulf Coast. The South contains a Piedmont, Tidewater, Appalachia, Ozarks, Coastal Plains, Alluvial Lowlands, Everglades Swamp, and Mississippi Delta. A myriad of rivers cross the region, including the Potomac, Rappahannock, Cumberland, Chattahoochee, Appalachicola, and of course Mississippi. Yet within this topographic diversity exists a shared understanding that the South stretches from somewhere just north of the Chesapeake Bay to the southern-most point of the Florida Keys. It extends west into Arkansas, Texas, and perhaps to Missouri and Oklahoma.

The American South, however, has not been borne of simply geographic space. The region has also been a historical entity. In large part, the American South owes its creation to the seventeenth-century decision of Virginian tobacco planters to import African-American slaves. The development of chattel slavery has shaped the history of the American South, as have the tobacco, rice and cotton plantations on which slaves labored. After the American Revolution, as Northern states gradually abandoned the use of unfree labor, the connection between slavery and geography became more pronounced. The nation divided into "free states" and "slave states," with the latter being used in lieu of the term "Southern states." Slavery did not completely define the South, but the South cannot be defined without it.

The American Civil War also undeniably defined the South. The war created heroes, a mythology, a history, a nationality, and a formal geographic entity. Without doubt, the eleven Confederate states sealed their position within the American South by virtue of their decisions to secede from the United States in 1861. Few can doubt the "Southernness" of Alabama, Arkansas, Florida, Georgia, Louisiana, Mississippi, North Carolina, South Carolina, Tennessee, Texas, and Virginia. All contained sizable slave populations, and they all joined the Confederacy to protect this economic and cultural interest. Membership rights in the American South are less clear in regard

The Southern states

the Southern states as defined in this atlas

0   300 km

0   300 miles

to Maryland, Delaware, Kentucky, and Missouri. These antebellum slaveholding states placed themselves on the margins of the American South by virtue of their adherence to the Union during the American Civil War.

Since the end of the war, the South has struggled with the issues that resulted from the history of slavery and emancipation. Southern states have sizable black populations, underdeveloped industries, high poverty and homicide rates, low suicide rates, and large rural populations. In addition, the region contains distinct dialects, foods, ideas about education, and gender expectations. There are also regional distinctions in architecture, literature, music, recreation, and religion. Because of this cultural definition, many African-Americans consider themselves to be Southerners, even as they reside in Chicago, New York City, or Los Angeles. They continue to eat Southern foods, speak with a Southern accent, and call themselves Southerners. In the twentieth century, the United States census included West Virginia, Oklahoma, and the District of Columbia in its definition of the America South. The logic of this inclusion was that each of these states embodied many of the cultural traits that have defined the modern South. They had large African-American populations, they often followed the dictates of Jim Crow segregation, and many of their residents self-consciously declared themselves to be Southerners.

Roughly speaking, the history of the American South splits into five chronological parts. The seventeenth and eighteenth centuries (the Nascent South) were an era where the seeds of a regional identity and culture were germinating but not yet coherent. Tobacco, indentured servants, the emergence of race slavery, and interactions with Native-Americans define this era. A coherent region (the Antebellum South) came into maturity around 1820. Cotton plantations, African-American slaves, westward expansion, and yeoman farmers defined this antebellum era. During these decades, Southerners and Northerners became increasingly dissimilar and these sectional differences took center stage in national politics. The next era (the Confederate South) came into existence in 1861, when eleven Southern states seceded from the United States and initiated the American Civil War. This third period, filled perhaps with the most drama, came to an end when Robert E. Lee surrendered at Appomattox in April, 1865, and the Confederate States of America disintegrated. The Southern nation may have been destroyed on the battlefield, but its memory continued to shape the region for the generations that followed. This fourth era (the New South) began under Reconstruction and continued for approximately eighty years. Urbanization, industrialization, and progressive reforms characterized these decades. Despite the struggle to restructure the society, many of the antebellum characteristics persisted through the twentieth century. This New South displayed many of the same themes that made the Old South a distinct region. Slavery was replaced by sharecropping, and slave codes by black codes. Finally, Franklin Delano Roosevelt's New Deal initiated the fifth stage of the region's history (the Modern South), one characterized by a diminishing of regionalism in the nation. The South continues to exist, but the New Deal,

Civil Rights Movement, and forces of modernization have altered the regional character. The South became increasingly American; or perhaps America became increasingly Southern.

Over the past five hundred years, the American South has undergone dramatic transformations. It has witnessed the European settlement of the Atlantic shore, the decimation and then forced removal of various Indian peoples, the introduction and cultivation of staple products such as tobacco, rice, and cotton, the rise and fall of African-American slavery, the westward expansion of American settlement, the creation of a Southern Nation, and the gradual emergence of industry, cities, and racial tolerance. Throughout all this, the idea of the American South has persisted, and the region has maintained itself as a culture area, geographic expression, and historical entity unto itself. It is to these trends, events, and themes that we now turn.

Thomas James, a British officer, mapped Charles Town Harbor during the siege that ended in the surrender of American rebel forces in May 1780. In this marshy estuary one can see scattered country seats on plots of slightly higher ground and numerous waterways that could be used for communication. Indigo was grown successfully after a first experiment with seeds imported from Antigua in 1742. Sullivans Island, off the North Channel, was used as a quarantine for arriving slaves.

PART I: THE NASCENT SOUTH

The roots of the American South were planted long before the Confederacy was formed or cotton plantations littered the region. Indeed, a Southern culture existed before the arrival of European settlers in the seventeenth century. The Native Americans indigenous to the southeastern corner of North America shared what archeologists have called the Southeastern Ceremonial Complex. Although the native groups in the region spoke different languages and often waged war against each other, they shared religious beliefs, symbols, customs, and costumes. These inhabitants, who were mostly horticulturists, built enormous earthen mounds as burial grounds, temple mounts, and ceremonial centers. They lived largely in small cities and in hierarchical chiefdoms. These chiefdoms—which included the Coosa, Altamaha, Apalachee, Talisi, and Alibamo—contained powerful chiefs, institutions of centralized power, specialized labor forces, intricate systems of tribute, and sophisticated agricultural practices. Even after the introduction of European diseases largely destroyed these peoples, an Indian presence continued to shape the development of the American South.

The European settlement of the American South occurred in piecemeal fashion. In 1607, London's Virginia Company began the first successful attempt by the English to colonize. Their settlement, Jamestown, struggled to survive in its early years. Tobacco horticulture and indentured servitude provided an avenue for economic prosperity for the colony, but local Algonquian Indians prevented true stability. After a series of bloody Anglo-Powhatan wars, Virginians finally obtained control of the region in the late seventeenth century. The other Chesapeake colony, Maryland, began with a land grant to George Calvert, who wished to establish a settlement of Roman Catholics. This colony also became quickly wedded to tobacco, and like Virginia, it faced a labor shortage in the early 1660s. By 1670, planters throughout the Chesapeake relied on the labor of African slaves. Further south, English refugees from Barbados settled South Carolina in the 1680s. There, the cultivation of indigo and the deerskin trade brought a modicum of economic stability. Slave laborers eventually harvested a profitable rice crop, and in 1708 South Carolina had the South's first and only black majority. Four years later, the less prosperous North Carolina officially separated from South Carolina. In 1733, James Oglethorpe established Georgia, the last of the English colonies in the southeast. At first this colony appeared quite different from its neighbors, as its Board of Trustees designed it as a moral experiment. The colony initially banned African slavery, forbade the use of rum and other liquors, and severely restricted trade with the Indians. These bans would not last long, as colonists defied them from the outset. The English were not the only Europeans to colonize the American South. French and Spanish settlers occupied most of the Gulf Coast, including Florida and the lower Mississippi Valley. There, the French and Spanish vied for the allegiances and trade of neighboring Native Americans, built garrisons and missions, and otherwise established permanent settlements.

Beneath the diversity of the Southern colonies lie several themes that affiliated them with each other and with the more unified American South that appeared in the early nineteenth century. First, each of the Southern colonies confronted and competed with various Native and European nations for a sustained period of time. Native Americans and European settlers traded with one another, fought wars against each other, intermarried, created diplomatic alliances, and borrowed cultural traits from each other. This experience did not completely separate Southern colonies from those to the north. However, in the southeast, the confrontation between Natives and European newcomers was sustained over a much longer period. Where most New Englanders believed that the local Indians had either disappeared or been pacified by the end of the seventeenth century, Southerners dealt with the Five Civilized Tribes well into the nineteenth century. Even the history of forced removal in the 1830s did not eliminate the ability of some Cherokees, Creeks, Choctaws, and Chickasaws to fight for the Confederacy in the 1860s.

A reliance on the cultivation of a range of staple products also united the Southern colonies. In the Chesapeake region, tobacco provided a means for hopeful planters to recoup their early losses. In the Carolinas, indigo, deerskins, and later rice allowed the colony to flourish. Georgians found deerskins and rice to be their most important export crops.

Finally, all of the Southern colonies used systems of unfree labor to fulfill their labor needs. Indentured servants from England and Ireland provided most of the labor during the first sixty years of English settlement in the American South. After the 1660s, African slaves became the predominant choice of landowners for labor. Even Georgia quickly abandoned its restriction against slavery. This transition sealed the future of a multiracial South. South Carolina's black majority was not replicated in the other Southern colonies, but by the American Revolution slave populations had steadily increased in all of them.

The colonial South resembled its antebellum counterparts in numerous other ways. Both societies were violent, racist, patriarchal, dispersely settled, and rural. Most white residents lived as yeoman farmers or small independent planters, and most African-Americans served as slaves on staple crop plantations. Political leaders in both eras received their privilege by birth, and the colonial varieties of labor systems paralleled those that would follow. Nevertheless, the American South in the seventeenth and eighteenth centuries was still in the process of maturing. Little or no sense of a Southern consciousness existed in the colonial era, and during these formative years the territorial limits of the South constantly changed. Yet the seventeenth and eighteenth centuries contain hints of the Old South that would later flourish.

Shell gorget from the Southeastern Ceremonial Complex, c. A.D. 1000. A flying shaman with wings and talons of a bird of prey holds a human head in one hand.

The Mound Builders

Major mounds

▲ Adena or Hopewell mound, 1000 B.C.–A.D. 1000

▲ Mississipian mound, A.D. 700–1700

When European explorers traveled into the North American interior during the sixteenth century, they stumbled upon undeniable proof of ancient civilizations. Hernando de Soto, for example, encountered several large man-made earthen mounds during his journeys into the southeastern interior in 1539 to 1543. Later, in the eighteenth century, naturalist William Bartram observed that Cherokee Indians occupied some of these mounds. These structures filled the countryside west of the Appalachian Mountains and south of the Ohio Valley. Some were so large that their full size could not be determined until the advent of twentieth-century aerial reconnaissance. In size alone, these mounds impressed upon its visitors proof of a powerful and advanced people.

In the years that followed De Soto's travels, the earthen mounds in the southeast served as the focus of wonderfully imaginative myths and misperceptions. By the nineteenth century, Americans posited countless explanations for the presence of the mounds. Scholars and clergymen proclaimed that they had been built by one of many ancient groups, including the Egyptians, Trojans, Welsh, Norsemen, Spaniards, or even the survivors of the Lost Continent of Atlantis. Similarly, the Book of Mormon and other religious texts declared that the builders descended from the ten Lost Tribes of Israel. Some theorists insisted on the Aztec origins of the mounds. Rarely, however, were the Native Americans indigenous to the southeast seen as responsible for these remnants of a past civilization. They were believed to be too disorganized, uneducated, and uncivilized to build something so elaborate and technically sophisticated.

Modern scholars have dismissed the earlier myths about Indians that prevented their connection to the building of the mounds. Not surprisingly, modern archeologists have learned that the mounds were built by earlier generations of Indians hundreds of years before contact. Most of the Natives who built these mounds shared what is known as the Southeastern Ceremonial Complex, a group of shared religious beliefs and symbols held by many of the southeastern Mississippian people in the prehistoric period. Artifacts such as pottery and gorgets confirm that southeastern Indians shared similar ceremonial costumes, objects, and symbols. Many of these symbols are similar to those used in Mesoamerica and are associated with agriculture and fertility. The most pervasive of these symbols is a cross enclosed in a circle. Other symbols include swastikas, feathered serpents, human hands with eyes, circles with scalloped edges, spirals, human skulls, and forked eyes. The human figures depicted in the Southeastern Ceremonial Complex wear ear spools, necklaces made of conch shells, hair knots, tasseled belts, and aprons. The prehistoric southeastern peoples, although disparate in the languages they spoke and the structures of their societies, built the mounds in similar painstaking fashion—one basket of dirt at a time.

The peoples indigenous to the eastern part of North America built their earthen structures over a period of three thousand years. Many of the oldest mounds, built in the Woodland tradition (1000 B.C. to A.D. 700), served as burial sites. Some of the mounds built in the Mississippian tradition (A.D. 700 to A.D. 1700) served as foundations for the Native American's most important buildings. Most of these mounds were finished by A.D. 1300. They supported temples, mortuaries, and houses of powerful chiefs. Natives palisaded some mounds, built them near important waterways, and defended them with ditches and towers. Some mounds were rather isolated while others appeared to be precisely positioned with neighboring ones. Several had exact geometric dimensions, with circle-, square- or octagon-shaped embankments.

Occasionally, Natives built the mounds in clusters which became the ceremonial center for large chiefdoms. Perhaps the most impressive site is Cahokia. Located in present day Collinsville, Illinois, it served as the region's largest ceremonial and population center. Built around A.D. 700 and occupied for almost 600 years, Cahokia covered 5 1/2 square miles and housed nearly forty thousand inhabitants. It contained 22,000,000 cubic feet of earth, and the base of the structure was larger than the Great Pyramid of Egypt. Among the spectacular findings at this site, archeologists unearthed surveying equipment, proof that a wooden palisade of over twenty thousand logs encircled the entire site, and elite burial grounds. In addition, the mounds often included pottery, trophy skulls, a diversity of tools, baskets, gorgets, body adornments, smoking pipes, stone tablets, and animal masks. Monks Mound, a giant pyramid, stood in the center of the Cahokia complex. It rose 100 feet and had a base of 1,040 by 790 feet. Without question, Cahokia and the other mounds prove the vitality of the peoples and cultures that were destroyed by European contact.

Cahokia, as it may have looked about 1,000 years ago.

Indians and the Arrival of Europeans

In 1540, a southeastern chief struggled to describe what the arrival of Europeans meant to his people. "The things that seldom happen bring astonishment. Think, then, what must be the effect on me and mine, the sight of you and your people, whom we have at no time seen, stride the fierce brutes, your horses, entering with such speed and fury into my country, that we had no tidings of your coming." "Astonishment," he admitted, hardly approached the impact of what had happened. In the decades that preceded and followed this statement, the lives of Native Americans were turned completely upside down. Europeans may have "discovered" a New World in 1492, but the peoples that lived there for the past millennia watched their "old world" change so dramatically that it became a new world to them as well.

Before the sustained arrival of Europeans in the sixteenth century, an ethnic and cultural mosaic of nations and tribes covered the Americas. Internal differences outweighed any notion of a shared "Indian" heritage. The southeastern part of North America contained dozens of distinct chiefdoms. These complex Mississippian societies, which had formed several centuries earlier, generally contained paramount chiefs, hierarchical structures, institutions of centralized power, and specialized labor forces. These groups of southeastern Indians relied heavily on agricultural production, held diverse cosmologies, and competed for power and territory as distinct political entities. On the northern fringes of the southeast, near the Chesapeake Bay, lived somewhat smaller groups of Algonquian Indians. Like their southern neighbors, these Native peoples lived in towns governed by chiefs and practiced a combination of horticulture, foraging, and fishing. Unlike the Natives further south,

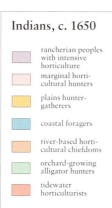

Indians, c. 1650

- rancherian peoples with intensive horticulture
- marginal horticultural hunters
- plains hunter-gatherers
- coastal foragers
- river-based horticultural chiefdoms
- orchard-growing alligator hunters
- tidewater horticulturists

however, they spoke languages from the Algonquian family and formed no large chiefdoms before European contact. Nothing united these diverse groups of indigenous peoples into a single entity. They spoke different languages, fought wars against each other, captured prisoners, and believed themselves to be different peoples and from superior civilizations. Only after the arrival of European explorers and colonists, and the tumultuous demographic consequences that ensued, did these disparate peoples become "Indians."

Pomeiockt, North Carolina. Between 1585 and 1587, while he was staying on Roanoke Island, John White made this watercolor representing the small Native American town located at the mouth of Gibbs Creek.

The population of North America at the time of European contact continues to elude precise assessment, but the population within the present United States in 1491 probably hovered around seven million. North America was not, as has been asserted, "virgin land" before the arrival of the European newcomers. The years that followed contact brought countless and dramatic changes for every Indian nation. Most important, they faced epidemics that ravaged their communities. Smallpox, measles, bubonic plague, and influenza reduced the population of the Indians of the southeast to a mere quarter of a million within a century. Indians had few effective responses to the diseases for which they had no immunity. Some ethnic populations were completely wiped out, while remnants of other communities struggled to survive. Epidemics continued to plague native communities long after the initial disruptions of contact. Georgia and Florida Timucuan-speakers and Texas Coahuiltecan-speakers, for example, survived the early waves of disease. But by the time of the American Revolution almost three centuries after contact, new waves of epidemics had wiped them out.

Demographic disruptions irrevocably altered Native societies. Smaller populations could not support the elaborate systems of tribute that characterized the pre-Columbian chiefdoms. In response to the changes, the Native societies of the southeast simplified. They discarded their hierarchical structures, altered their settlement patterns, ceased to have specialized crafts, and stopped performing many of their elaborate spiritual rituals. Out of this chaos came new Indian identities and political structures. The so-called Five Civilized Tribes—the Creeks, Choctaws, Chickasaws, Cherokees, and Seminoles—all formed during the tumultuous years after contact. Many Indian communities moved their villages inland to try to escape the unseen killers.

In the years that followed, these southeastern Indians continued to shape their world to fit the demands of European trade and a new diplomatic environment. For Indians in the southeast, this meant trading deerskins for guns, signing treaties and fighting wars with European powers, adopting European goods into Native villages, and facing Christian missionaries bent on saving them from their "savagery." This colonial South was built on the backs of the pre-Columbian ruins, but its character was unlike anything the Indians had seen before.

The Seeds of the South

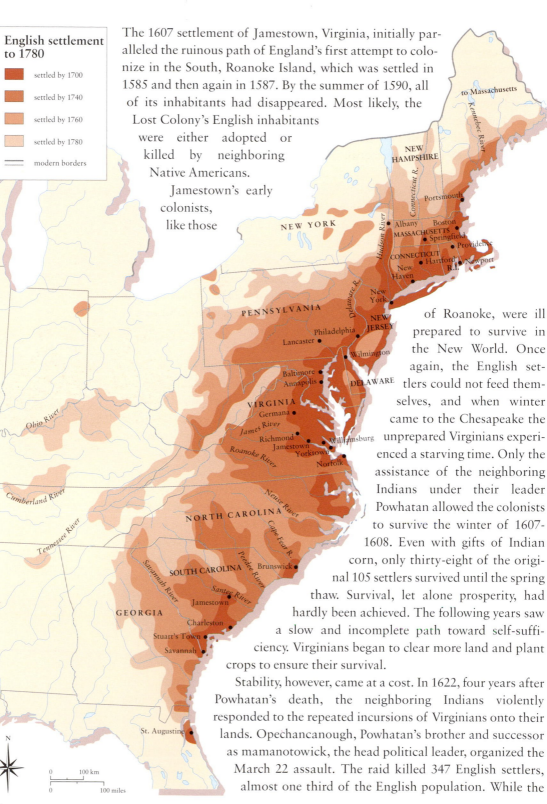

English settlement to 1780

- settled by 1700
- settled by 1740
- settled by 1760
- settled by 1780
- modern borders

The 1607 settlement of Jamestown, Virginia, initially paralleled the ruinous path of England's first attempt to colonize in the South, Roanoke Island, which was settled in 1585 and then again in 1587. By the summer of 1590, all of its inhabitants had disappeared. Most likely, the Lost Colony's English inhabitants were either adopted or killed by neighboring Native Americans.

Jamestown's early colonists, like those of Roanoke, were ill prepared to survive in the New World. Once again, the English settlers could not feed themselves, and when winter came to the Chesapeake the unprepared Virginians experienced a starving time. Only the assistance of the neighboring Indians under their leader Powhatan allowed the colonists to survive the winter of 1607-1608. Even with gifts of Indian corn, only thirty-eight of the original 105 settlers survived until the spring thaw. Survival, let alone prosperity, had hardly been achieved. The following years saw a slow and incomplete path toward self-sufficiency. Virginians began to clear more land and plant crops to ensure their survival.

Stability, however, came at a cost. In 1622, four years after Powhatan's death, the neighboring Indians violently responded to the repeated incursions of Virginians onto their lands. Opechancanough, Powhatan's brother and successor as mamanotowick, the head political leader, organized the March 22 assault. The raid killed 347 English settlers, almost one third of the English population. While the

Indians could claim initial victories, they did not achieve their ultimate goal of eliminating the English presence in the region. The community experienced heavy losses in the months of English retaliatory raids that followed. Although the following decades contained periods of tenuous peace between Powhatan's descendants and their English neighbors, tensions and hostilities irrevocably changed their relation to one another. Where only a few years earlier Virginians had turned to the Indians for their survival, they now primarily conceived of Indians as barriers to their prosperity.

The early settlers had not included tobacco in their plans, but the colony quickly became dependent on this "dirty sot weed." The first shipment of tobacco left Virginia in 1617. When it attracted an unexpected high price of three shillings a pound in England, Virginians quickly planted the new crop wherever they could. In 1620, Virginians shipped 60,000 pounds of tobacco across the Atlantic, and the growth that followed was exponential. A decade later, Virginians shipped 350,000 pounds of tobacco to England, and in 1640 they shipped over 1,000,000 pounds. Virginians had found the means to obtain the prosperity that originally brought them to the fledgling colony. Thousands of Englishmen hoped to share in this bounty.

A detail from John Ferrar's map of Virginia, 1651.

The growing demands for tobacco resulted in growing demands for labor. Although twenty Africans arrived in Virginia in 1619, Virginians did not rely on race slavery until decades later. Instead, white indentured servants provided most of the unfree labor in the first half of the seventeenth century. Thousands of Englishmen pledged years of service (usually seven) in return for free passage to the Virginia colony. The restrictive expense of the transatlantic passage, which cost the equivalent of a year's-worth of labor for an English servant or laborer, led most prospective colonists to enter into this type of agreement. The hopes of free land and economic prosperity made indentured servitude desirable and attractive. Those who survived their indentures often became landowners and masters themselves. As the first half of the seventeenth century progressed, the demands for labor skyrocketed in the Chesapeake.

By the 1670s, the supply of willing indentured servants could not keep pace with the ever-growing demands for labor. English laborers watched as opportunities to obtain land became more limited in Virginia, and they sought out better opportunities in English colonies other than Virginia. The presence of race slavery in the Caribbean and West Indies, as well as the existence of a vibrant Atlantic slave trade, made the increased use of African slaves a natural decision for the prospering Virginia planters. Virginians initially believed that the black bondsmen would compare unfavorably to their white servant counterparts. But when the colony's labor needs demanded a permanent workforce, African slaves fit the bill. Tobacco and slaves now provided the means for sustained growth in the region and provided incentive for Virginians to settle and cultivate the hunting grounds of neighboring Indians. With tobacco, Virginians had planted the seeds of Southern society.

Importing Black America

In 1619, Virginian John Rolfe, a tobacco planter and recent widower of Pocahontas, wrote that "about the last of August came a Dutch man of war that sold us twenty negroes." Although few Virginians recorded this historic moment, the arrival of twenty Africans to Jamestown marked the beginning of black America. The rise of a slave South, however, occurred slowly. In 1680, six decades after the initial arrival of black immigrants, African-Americans formed only seven percent of Virginia's non-Indian population. By 1750, this population had skyrocketed to forty-four percent. During the same period, South Carolina went from a population of seventeen percent slave to a black majority (sixty-one percent slave). The labor demanded by tobacco, rice, and cotton cultivation created an institution of slavery that defined the region for generations.

The earliest slaves in America arrived through the Atlantic slave trade, which had its roots in Africa, where rival kingdoms enslaved war captives generations before the arrival of Europeans. Prior to the demand for slaves in the New World, these slaves served in a system that greatly differed from what evolved in the Americas. Generalizing about slavery in Africa is rather difficult; the continent contained diverse cultures, and each culture's unique slave system changed over time. A few traits, however, characterized most African systems and made them different from those in the Americas. Most slaves in Africa could legally marry, buy their own freedom, obtain an education, and practice their own religions. Masters in Africa frequently manumitted their slaves, the occupations that slaves held were diverse (soldiers, field workers, concubines, government officials, etc.), and slavery was assumed to be a status that could befall anyone. There was no connection between race or skin color and slavery in Africa. Until the sixteenth century, almost all African slaves served African masters.

The labor demands of the recently colonized Americas brought a different option to Africa: slavery in the New World. In the sixteenth century, demanding European slave traders began to shape African traditions of the system to their labor needs. They offered guns and supplies to African rulers who subsequently provided the Europeans with captives of war or slaves. In addition, traders occasionally threatened rulers who refused to participate in the new transatlantic labor market. Soon, most African slaves ceased to serve African masters. In addition, some African nations began to wage war solely to obtain captives. Selling slaves to European slavers became a profitable business for some Africans.

Slave trade, mid 18th century

═══	modern borders
──	Proclamation Line, 1763
➤	slave trade route
●	slave port

from Africa, South America, Latin America, and the Caribbean

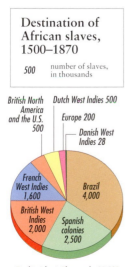

Destination of African slaves, 1500–1870

500   number of slaves, in thousands

British North America and the U.S. 500

Dutch West Indies 500

Europe 200

Danish West Indies 28

French West Indies 1,600

British West Indies 2,000

Spanish colonies 2,500

Brazil 4,000

Total in Atlantic Slave trade: 11,328

The business of slave trading occurred in the slave markets along the western coast of Africa. These slave markets and ports were where Africans and Europeans primarily interacted. Each slave port had its own reputation. Some ports had better prices, more slaves, safer weather, and better security. Some ports earned reputations for having more docile or aggressive slaves, and others sold slaves from ethnic groups that were especially sought after by American colonists. The European slavers were very aware of these intricacies of their occupation.

The journey from freedom in Africa to slavery in America was a horrific one. The three-thousand-mile sea voyage to the Americas—the Middle Passage—extracted a cost beyond human comprehension. In sheer numbers alone, the Middle Passage was the defining moment for many Africans. From 1500 to 1808, over eleven million Africans survived this upheaval. The journeys brought Africans and slavery to every region Europeans inhabited in the Americas. Only a small proportion—about 500,000—of these slaves arrived in the British North America. By the Civil War, these initial African imports had multiplied to nearly four million slaves. Other countries and colonies imported many more. Brazil, the country which imported nearly forty percent of all slaves from Africa, brought in over 250,000 slaves between 1836 and 1840.

The terror of the Middle Passage was determined by conditions below deck—not merely by the extent of its results. Numbers of slaves alone cannot account for the total horror of the experience. Death, disease, and malnutrition threatened anyone who took the typical two-month sea voyage. Slaves suffered from starvation, endured sea sickness, and struggled in horrific sanitary conditions. At least twenty percent of all Africans placed on ships bound for the Americas died during the journey. Some journeys extracted even higher costs. Ships were tightly packed, slaves were frequently chained together, and white crewmen constantly oversaw the slave's actions.

Surviving the Middle Passage normally resulted in a lifetime of slavery. Some slaves committed suicide on the ships rather than succumb to such a fate, while others plotted revolts to turn the ships back to Africa. Most African slaves, however, had neither the means nor the opportunity for such resistance. Still, the slave trade did not necessarily destroy the spirits of those who endured it. Instead, with the arrival of African slaves a vibrant African-American culture appeared on the farms and plantations of the American South.

Slave trade in Africa, mid 18th century

main area of origin of slaves

TEKE   supplier tribe

→   slave trade route

Main European forts

British
Danish
Dutch
French
Portuguese
other

From Africans to African-Americans

Black population

In percentage of total
population (estimates)

- 61
- 25
- 10
- 4
- 0

1680

0   100 km

0   100 miles

N

NEW HAMPSHIRE

MASSACHUSETTS

NEW YORK

CON.

R. I.

PENNSYLVANIA

NEW JERSEY

MARYLAND

DELAWARE

VIRGINIA

NORTH CAROLINA

SOUTH CAROLINA

GEORGIA

The Atlantic slave trade brought peoples from diverse African cultures to the Americas. Most slaves came from one of three geographical and cultural groupings in West Africa: Upper Guinea, Lower Guinea, and the Angola Coast. As many as fifty distinct languages were spoken and each grouping contained distinct religions, cultural practices, and political systems. Although the Middle Passage created a common experience among the enslaved Africans—whether they were ethnically Ibo, Angola, Asante, Callabard, Gambian, Dahomean, Fanti-Ashanti, or Yoruba—it did not fully erase the cultural divisions that existed in Africa. Ethnic diversity was transported in chains to the American colonies. Newly formed slave communities were split by linguistic, religious, and social divisions. The continued importation of African slaves perpetuated ethnic divisions until the eighteenth century. Even so, trends toward a creolized African-American culture began on the slave ships and continued in the slave quarters. Only after sustained interaction in the Americas did a unified African or African-American identity emerge.

In the 1720s and 1730s, enslaved Africans in mainland British North America began to experience a phenomenon that was not replicated by any other enslaved community in the Americas—growth by natural increase. As the slave population slowly began to grow through natural increase, American-born slaves began to outnumber those who were being imported. The Atlantic slave trade continued for nearly a century after this phenomenon became apparent to Southern slaveholders, and births increasingly contributed to the region's growing slave population. When the United States conducted its first census in 1790, natural increase and African imports combined to create a slave population of nearly 700,000. The decision of the United States to end its participation in the Atlantic slave trade in 1808 did nothing to stop this population explosion. In 1860, a nation that had imported only approximately 500,000 Africans over the past two and a half centuries contained nearly four million African-American slaves.

An American-born slave population had ramifications for the slaves as well as for those who owned them. For starters, it allowed the cultural diversity within slave communities to become less pronounced. As the American-born population grew, many slaves were born into communities that had taken the initial steps toward creating an African-American culture. These children did not have to repeat the steps of their parents, because they were socialized into this ever-changing culture. This further increased the trends toward linguistic, religious, cultural, and social homogeneity. Adapted to the New World and the neighboring European and Indian cultures, African-American culture also retained many of its African roots. This culture encompassed religion, naming patterns, ideas about time, music, dancing, folk tales, foods, kinship, and language.

The ramifications extended beyond the creation of an African-American culture. Southern masters now enjoyed the economic benefits of a self-reproducing labor force and received a new economic rationale for recognizing slave families and encouraging slave marriages. Colonial and state laws did not protect, let alone condone, marital relationships between slaves. Many masters, however, recognized slave families by building them separate quarters and even by attending informal weddings. Even when masters did not explicitly recognize marriages, they rarely forbade their slaves from sexual relationships. Slave marriages and sexual couplings were too great an investment for masters. Southern slaveholders recognized that second-generation slaves were born with immunities to many of the deadly European-born diseases, were immediately socialized into a slave community, and helped balance the community's sex ratio. Slave families, therefore, served the desires of both slave and master alike.

A generation after the slave trade came to an end, former slave Charles Ball asserted that the transition to an American-born slave community profoundly affected the slave community. Unlike those born in America, he wrote, the African imports usually "feel indignant at the servitude that is imposed upon them, and only want power to inflict the must cruel retribution upon their oppressors. . . . They are universally of the opinion, and this is founded in their religion, that after death they shall return to their own country, and rejoin their former companions and friends." Ball echoed what Southern masters learned a century earlier; slaves with local families were less willing to run away or risk the ramifications of participating in large-scale revolts. This result of the self-perpetuating African-American population brought a new level of stability to the South's "peculiar institution."

1770

NEW HAMPSHIRE

MASSACHUSETTS

NEW YORK

CON.

R. I.

PENNSYLVANIA

NEW JERSEY

MARYLAND

DELAWARE

VIRGINIA

NORTH CAROLINA

SOUTH CAROLINA

GEORGIA

0   100 km

0   100 miles

Diversity in Early America

This map of St. Augustine, appeared in 1766 in William Stork's Description of East Florida, *as the town had just been acquired by the English. The town enjoyed a sheltered position, with the recently built Fort San Marcos guarding a narrow entrance between the coast and Anastasia Island (not represented here).*

In 1785, Thomas Jefferson, himself a Virginian, outlined the differences between Northerners and Southerners. "In the North they are cool, sober, laborious, independent, jealous of their own liberties, and just to those of others, interested, chicaning, superstitious and hypocritical . in their religion." Southerners, the future President insisted, were quite different. "They are fiery, voluptuary, indolent, unsteady, zealous for their own liberties, but trampling on those of others, generous, candid, without attachment or pretensions to any religion but that of the heart." Jefferson may have oversimplified what divided the young republic, but he perceptively described the presence of a pervasive feature of the American landscape: regional cultures.

Only decades earlier, the South was hardly a region at all and no one spoke of a people called Southerners. Prior to the American Revolution, internal distinctions divided the colonies that later formed the South and prevented outbursts of regional identification. Nationalities and loyalties splintered the southeast into a virtual mosaic. Some parts of Florida were under Spanish rule and some under British rule. Similarly, the French governed New Orleans and the Louisiana Territory. The other Southern colonies were under British rule, but were largely governed by local elites with provincial concerns. Creeks, Choctaws, Chickasaws, Cherokees, and Seminoles controlled most of what is now Florida, Alabama, Mississippi, Tennessee, Kentucky, Arkansas, and Missouri. Native American nations also occupied much of the land that the British claimed as their possession in Georgia, South Carolina, North Carolina, and Virginia.

Internal divisions extended beyond national loyalties and issues of territorial control. Within the Southern colonies, agrarian distinctions divided British settlers as much as they united them. In the era before cotton, Georgia, South Carolina, North Carolina, Virginia, and Maryland grew indigo, sugar, rice, wheat, corn, and tobacco. The Chesapeake region, which developed in accordance with the dictates of tobacco cultivation, contrasted sharply with the Lower South. There, in the Carolinas and Georgia, colonists harvested rice, indigo, and deerskins. The region's backcountry contained a volatile mix of Indian traders, herders, squatters, and small farmers. In terms of agriculture, there were at least three distinct Souths. Even within a single agricultural region, differences seemed to outweigh similarities. Catholic Maryland, for example, contrasted sharply with its Anglican Virginia neighbor. In addition to competing religious foundations, they had different economic and social structures.

Perhaps the only thing that the Southern colonies shared before 1776 was their commitment to the institution of African slavery. Slavery did not initially create a unified and distinct South, however. In its early stages the commitment to slavery was shared by the Northern colonies, which actively participated in the Atlantic slave trade and held slaves in bondage. South Carolina, which had a slave majority by 1708, contrasted sharply with neighboring Georgia, which at first banned the importation of slaves. By the eve of the Revolution, however, the regional association with slavery had become more pronounced. At this point, slavery prospered in the Southern colonies and stagnated in the Northern ones. In 1770, the only Northern colony with an African-American population of over ten percent was New York (11.7%). Concurrently, Maryland (31.5%), Virginia (42.0%), North Carolina (35.3%), South Carolina (40.5%), and Georgia (45.2%) all had over thirty percent of their population enslaved.

When Northern states began to abolish slavery in the aftermath of the American Revolution, the South became increasingly unified around slavery and, consequently, became a distinct region. It was through this process, during the discussions about the meanings of the Revolution, that a Southern consciousness emerged. During the Stamp Act Crisis, Continental Congresses, and Constitutional Conventions regional distinctions entered the forefront of political thought. Northerners began the process of emancipating their slaves as they contemplated the contradictions within the revolutionary rhetoric of liberty and equality and the insistence upon the justice of slaveholding. At the same time, white Southerners usually insisted on their "freedom" to own slaves. This resulted in a widespread recognition that slavery had created two regional cultures. "It seemed now to be pretty well understood," James Madison observed, "that the real difference of interests lay, not between the large and the small but between the N[orthern] and South[er]n States. The institution of slavery and its consequences formed the line of discrimination." Out of the American Revolution emerged a Southern consciousness and regional identity that continued to redefine itself over the next two hundred years.

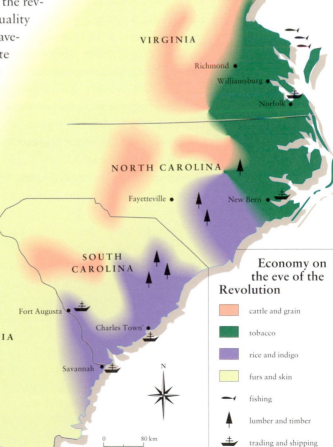

Economy on the eve of the Revolution

- cattle and grain
- tobacco
- rice and indigo
- furs and skin
- ⌁ fishing
- ▲ lumber and timber
- ⚓ trading and shipping

VIRGINIA

Richmond ●
Williamsburg ●
Norfolk ●

NORTH CAROLINA

Fayetteville ●   New Bern ●

SOUTH CAROLINA

Fort Augusta ⚓
Charles Town ●
GEORGIA
Savannah ⚓

N

0   80 km
0   80 miles

The Great Awakenings

In 1743, several Virginians in Hanover County stopped attending Sunday services at the official Anglican parish church. Instead, they began reading theological tracts and holding church meetings on their own. Led by Samuel Morris, a local bricklayer, they built a meetinghouse to accommodate their growing numbers and soon invited a New Light Presbyterian minister from the Virginia backcountry to lead their prayer meetings. With the arrival of William Robinson, these religious dissenters ceased being Anglicans. They now considered themselves Presbyterians and attracted large enthusiastic crowds and dozens of itinerant evangelical preachers. Similar revivals soon occurred throughout the backcountry and Tidewater region. Over the next three decades, waves of spiritual reawakenings swept over the Southern colonies. In addition to spreading Presbyterianism, by the 1760s these Awakenings established Methodism and Baptism at the forefront of Southern religion. A largely "unchurched" region found new spiritual guides.

Morris and his neighbors were inspired by the teachings of itinerant preacher George Whitefield, the assistant of Methodist founder John Wesley. Whitefield visited nearly all of the thirteen colonies in the eighteenth century. During his preaching tours of Virginia, the Carolinas, and Georgia, he sparked a series of religious revivals that offered an alternative to the structured Anglican norm. Whitefield sought to attract all Christians to this new conception of personal faith. "Don't tell me you are a Baptist, an Independent, a Presbyterian, a dissenter," he told the huge crowds of enthusiasts that gathered to watch him preach. "Tell me you are a Christian, that is all I want." Whitefield offered all of his listeners the idea of universal hope for salvation and the "free gift" of grace but warned them of a wrathful and omnipotent God. Inner conviction and an emotional connection to God, Whitefield preached, was more important than denomination. Salvation was available to everyone who took the opportunity, and damnation was for the rest. This was a change from the hierarchical

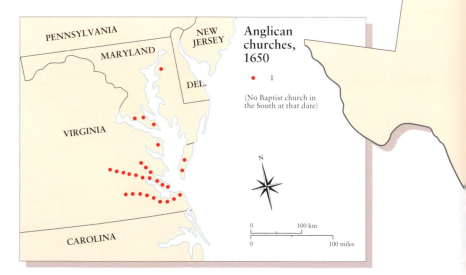

Anglican
churches,
1650

●   1

(No Baptist church in
the South at that date)

PENNSYLVANIA
NEW JERSEY
MARYLAND
DEL.
VIRGINIA
CAROLINA

0   100 km

0   100 miles

N

Anglican theology that stressed formal learning and the importance of ministers to mediate relationships with God.

Whitefield was a sight to see. He spoke in an inspired and booming voice, gestured violently, used biblical metaphors, and relied heavily on the vernacular. He preached totally from memory, thus giving him the appearance of divine inspiration. A facial tic made him appear cross-eyed, but this too reinforced the perception of his divine blessing. Whitefield sought and received emotional responses from many of the men and women who felt the "new light." His words and spiritual intensity brought audiences to tears and evoked shouts of repentance and remorse. Fainting was not uncommon. Many Americans considered him to be the greatest orator of his age. After witnessing a mob of 30,000 people crowding the streets of Philadelphia, religious skeptic Benjamin Franklin could only attest to the "extraordinary influence of his oratory." When the sermons ended, "it seem'd as if all the World were growing Religious; so that one could not walk thro' the Town in an Evening without Hearing Psalms sung in different Families of every Street." For some,

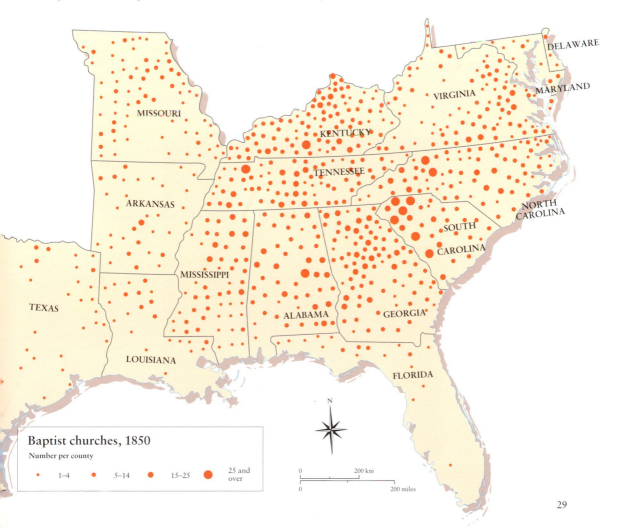

Baptist churches, 1850

Number per county

· 1–4   · 5–14   ● 15–25   ⬤ 25 and over

Whitefield was a wonderful performer. For others, he and other itinerant evangelical preachers offered salvation.

The Great Awakenings had far-reaching effects. Before the Awakenings of the 1740s, the Anglican Church had nearly a monopoly on religious loyalties in the Chesapeake region. Nonevangelical Protestant groups—Lutherans and Quakers—as well as Presbyterians and Baptists had some adherents further south, while small Jewish and Catholic communities were scattered in South Carolina, Georgia, and Maryland. Still, Anglicans held numerical superiority in every Southern colony. Many Southerners continued to be apathetic about religion and largely unchurched. In the aftermath of the Great Awakenings, churchgoers were reinvigorated and evangelical Protestant sects took their prominent places on the Southern landscape. Methodists, Presbyterians, and Baptists all benefited from the Awakenings. They attracted a cross section of Southern society in ways that the Anglican Church had not. The poor and enslaved found spiritual solace in the egalitarian ideas of brotherhood and sisterhood, and they rejoiced in their faith that salvation was a human, not divine, choice.

The South did more than accept the evangelical teachings of the Great Awakenings in the decades that followed. Over the next century, Methodists and Baptists came to dominate the region. Anglican, Catholic, and Jewish communities maintained their presence, but these groups watched as their region's character became an evangelical one. Just as the South embraced evangelicalism, the itinerant preachers embraced the South. Despite the egalitarian

A young minister from England, George Whitefield toured America during the mid-eighteenth century and became the most popular preacher of the Great Awakening.

and nonviolent roots of their faith, evangelicals eventually helped perpetuate a "Bible Belt" that was committed to the maintenance of slavery and adherence to a Southern code of honor. Evangelical leaders later led the proslavery movement, supported secession, and reinforced the region's conservative notion of traditional values.

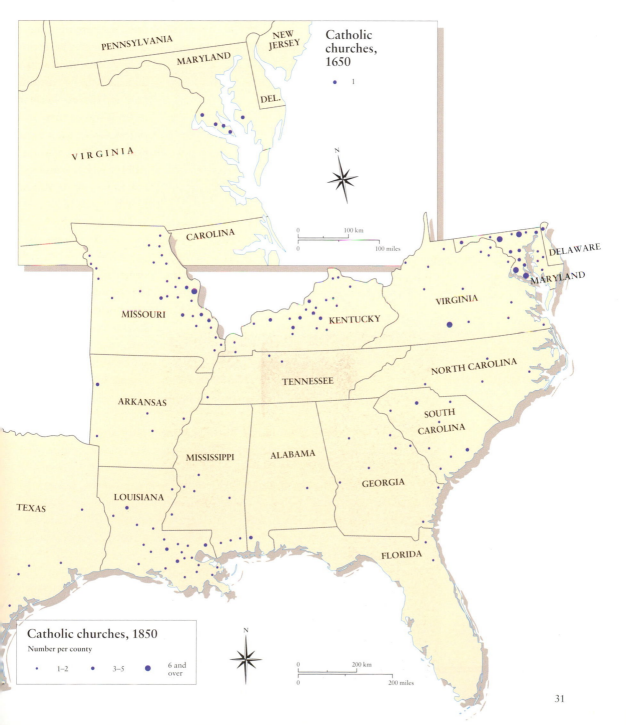

Catholic churches, 1650

•   1

Catholic churches, 1850

Number per county

•   1–2   •   3–5   ●   6 and over

The American Revolution in the South

Revolutionary battles in the South

- British army assembly area
- American army assembly area
- British advance
- American clearing operations, late 1781
- British outpost, 1781
- town still held by British, 1781
- British victory
- American victory

Even before the July 1776 Declaration of Independence, rebellious Southerners were fighting British troops. The first substantial military action in the region occurred a month earlier when the British launched a failed assault on Charles Town Harbor in South Carolina. For the next 2 1/2 years, however, the War of American Independence remained confined primarily to the northeast. It was not until 1778 that the British initiated a campaign specifically designed to confront the peculiar nature of Southern society. Great Britain sought to capture the agricultural strongholds of Virginia, North Carolina, South Carolina, and Georgia with the assistance of thousands of Southern loyalists. These supporters of the Crown, the British hoped, would help capture the region and later hold and administer it. In December, British General Henry Clinton with the assistance of General Charles Cornwallis launched the first successful campaign in the region by successfully taking Savannah, Georgia. As they had hoped, Southerners loyal to the Crown helped capture and occupy the Georgia port city. In addition to those loyalists who formally enlisted, the British army was aided by hundreds of African-American slaves who saw victory as a path toward freedom. Southern blacks unloaded equipment, erected barricades, and helped control the port.

The British planned on using loyalists to recapture the Southern interior. Scottish Highlanders in the backcountry lived in populous communities which remained loyal to the Crown. They volunteered to fight the rebels with the tactics of guerrilla warfare and terror. Similarly, the British also recognized the benefits of utilizing the South's enslaved population. They counted on African-American slaves to undermine and oppose the Revolutionary cause. Fighting for liberty became a literal enlistment device as countless slaves obtained their freedom in the British army. In 1776, over one thousand slaves fought for Lord Dunmore under the banner "Liberty to Slaves!" The British also believed that neighboring Native Americans would ally themselves against their ever-intrusive rebel neighbors. The Indians, they believed, would remain loyal to Britain, the nation that provided them essential trade goods. Although many southeastern Indian nations proclaimed neutrality for as long as they could, members of the Creeks, Cherokees, Choctaws and Chickasaws all eventually allied themselves with the British.

Henry Clinton's Southern strategy began with a series of successes. After occupying Savannah, Clinton turned inland to capture Augusta and then pacify all of Georgia. Supported by local loyalists—red, black, and white—Clinton then prepared to assault South Carolina. Clinton's siege of Charles Town began on April 1, 1780, and lasted until American General Benjamin Lincoln surrendered the city on May 12. With this victory Clinton handed over the Southern campaign to Lord Cornwallis. In August, Cornwallis followed Clinton's successes by routing American forces in Camden, South Carolina. With the British now controlling South Carolina, hundreds of African-American slaves fled to freedom in Florida, found refuge behind British lines, or joined the British army. Cornwallis believed himself to be on the path to victory.

By autumn, however, Patriot forces were reasserting their presence in the region. Commander of the Southern Army Nathanael Greene implemented a strategy of guerrilla warfare and began to recapture most of Georgia and South Carolina. Finally, after months of setbacks, over one thousand rebels attacked the British at Kings Mountain on October 7. The Southerners destroyed the British forces in a vicious campaign. Cornwallis moved west in order to reassert British control in the region, but, before he could act, British forces suffered defeat at Cowpens. On March 15, 1781, Cornwallis endured a bitter victory at Guilford Court House. Although he won the battle, his troops suffered heavy losses. One quarter of his men lay dead or seriously wounded. Cornwallis could do nothing but retreat and regroup in Wilmington, North Carolina.

General Nathanael Greene, son of a Northern Quaker, later commanded the Southern Army.

Two months later, when Cornwallis decided to invade Virginia, he all but sealed the Patriot victory in the South. At first, the British general launched a series of successful raids in Virginia, but by September, American forces outnumbered the British two to one. American General George Washington launched a counteroffensive that took Cornwallis by surprise. Outnumbered and outmaneuvered, the British were unable to retreat or obtain reinforcements. On October 19, 1781, Cornwallis surrendered at Yorktown, effectively ending the war. The British evacuation of the South was slow, as negotiations with the United States did not produce a final treaty until September 1783. In July 1782, British troops vacated Savannah and in December 1782, British troops finally evacuated from Charles Town.

The War of 1812

Relations between England and the United States remained strained in the decades after the American Revolution. War between France and Great Britain in 1793 further weakened British-American relations. British blockades of American ports—designed to prevent American merchants from helping the French—aroused the ire of Americans. After the war, Great Britain continued its policy of naval blockades, imposed strict trading restrictions, and stopped neutral vessels on the high seas in order to arrest army deserters. By 1810, outraged Southern and Western American congressmen defended the rights to the free seas and also claimed that the British were inciting Indian uprisings in the Great Lakes Region and in the Southern backcountry. Nothing short of the sovereignty and honor of the United States, they stated, were at issue. Finally, in June 1812, President James Madison asked Congress to declare war on England. Southern representatives, in the face of bitter New England opposition, overwhelmingly voted for the measure. Congress declared war on June 18, 1812.

Initially, the war remained confined to the North and the Great Lakes regions. These early campaigns—an invasion of Canada along three fronts—were disasters for the young nation. A series of withdrawals and surrenders, as well as an effective British blockade of American ports, left the United States demoralized. In 1814, the British launched a major offensive against the United States. On August 24, 1814, British regulars entered Washington, DC, burned both the White House and the Capital building, and forced President Madison and Congress to flee. In September, the British struck Baltimore, but without the same success. When Fort McHenry refused to fall, the British were not deterred. They turned their eyes toward obtaining a favorable treaty at Ghent and initiating an assault on New Orleans.

British optimism for a successful Southern campaign relied heavily on their Creek Indian supporters. Influenced by the Shawnee warrior Tecumseh's call for a pan-Indian alliance, so-called "Red Stick" Creeks struck Georgia and Alabama settlements with force. Creek victories at Burnt Corn and Fort Mims outraged American settlers but encouraged British forces. The Mims massacre resulted in the deaths of between 250 and 275 Americans, African-American slaves, and friendly Creek Indians. Newspapers precisely described how women and children were burned alive in the Fort's buildings. A general panic within the region ensued. In the weeks that followed, Southern fears were compounded by rumors that six or eight hundred settlers were indiscriminately slain at Mims, and that the British were inciting slave uprisings and arming African-American troops in the region.

Before he became a popular military leader, Andrew Jackson started his career as an Indian fighter. In 1828 he was elected President of the United States.

British and Creek successes in the South were short-lived. Tennessee soldiers under the leadership of Major General Andrew Jackson arranged alliances with factions of neighboring Indians, including an offshoot of Creek Indians that remained friendly to the interests of the United States. Together, they marched from Huntsville, Alabama, southward through the state, avenging the deaths of the women and children from Fort Mims and stopping the majority of Creeks before they could "be supported by their allies the British and Spaniards." A series of victories over the Red Stick Creeks led Jackson to the Horseshoe Bend on the Tallapoosa River. There Jackson and his forces defeated a Creek army of one thousand warriors. On August 9, 1814, in the aftermath of the war, Jackson forced all of the Creeks, including his allies, to sign the Treaty of Fort Jackson. Twenty-three million acres of land were ceded to the United States and the most potent military threat in the region was pacified.

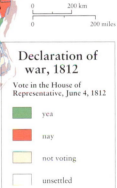

Victory over the Creeks did not end the War of 1812 but did change the direction that it took. British troops launched an offensive against New Orleans in December 1814, but General Jackson and his troops had arrived three weeks earlier to establish defensive fortifications. This massive military force—comprised of militiamen from Kentucky and Tennessee, free blacks from New Orleans, and allied Creeks—awaited the British. In early January, the long-anticipated assault began. Although the one-sided Battle of New Orleans lasted over an hour, the British army was torn apart in the first five minutes. When it was over, the Americans had only seventy-one casualties while the British suffered over two thousand.

The victory at the Battle of New Orleans secured Andrew Jackson's reputation as a soldier, created an explosion in nationalistic sentiment in the United States, and marked the end of the War of 1812. Less than a year earlier, many Americans and most New Englanders were inclined to sign an unfavorable peace treaty. The burning of the nation's capitol and defeats in the North seemed to indicate that the British remained an imperial force and the Americans were still in their infancy. Since then, a Southern general had subdued the hostile Creek Indians, opened up millions of acres of arable lands to Southern planters, and won a decisive victory over British invaders. The era of the Nascent South had ended and the antebellum era was born.

PART II: THE ANTEBELLUM SOUTH

*The "Old Red House,"
built in 1789 in North
Carolina, is a typical
example of the houses
that were built during the
eighteenth century in
much of the American
South. Tall and narrow,
they were one room deep
and two stories high,
with a full-length shed-
roof front porch and
a kitchen attached to
the back.*

Images of the Old South, or the antebellum South, abound in the popular imagination. Movies, television shows, and novelists depict an Old South filled with cotton, slavery, moonlight, and magnolias. However, the images of Dixie do not always agree with each other. While some assert that honorable gentlemen, compassionate mistresses, and subservient slaves resided in extravagant mansions on seemingly boundless cotton plantations, others show a darker side of reality. In the mythical world, glorified in *Gone With the Wind*, the rules of Southern hospitality governed an atmosphere of graciousness, and paternalistic masters protected their white and black families from any dangers that might appear. Our image of the South also includes the cruelty of slave punishments, the region's racist underpinnings, and its prevalence for violence. After all, the region stubbornly fought a war to preserve the oppressive system of slavery. African-American slaves, in this alternative image, stood ready to revolt at the slightest provocation, and the Underground Railroad brought a continuous stream of slaves to the promised land of freedom.

The reality of the Old South is more complex, and sometimes more mundane, than these two extremes would lead us to believe. The Old South not only contained wealthy planters, but also included impoverished yeoman farmers, struggling small planters, and a restless slave population that rarely risked completely rejecting its condition of bondage. Most planters struggled to pay off the debts accumulated in building their mansions and their reputations. A majority of the region's wealth was tied up in land and slaves, leaving luxuries and leisure in the hands of only a few. Even plantation mistresses had trouble fulfilling the roles expected of them. The myth of the pampered Southern lady could hardly be replicated in practice. The antebellum South was indeed "the land of cotton and slavery," but the implications of this phrase are not so straightforward.

The Old South, in all of its antebellum complexities, owed its existence to Eli Whitney and his creation of the cotton gin in 1783. Although this machine's importance to the region's culture would take decades to unfold, the ability to cultivate and market cotton at affordable prices radically transformed the South in the early nineteenth century. In fact, the Old South was the culmination of several trends that had their roots in the colonial era. During the nineteenth century, the American South expanded geographically, intensified its use of African-American slaves, witnessed the expansion of the Bible Belt, and saw the Northern states undergo an industrial transformation that made the regions even more distinct from each other. In each case, the cotton gin played an essential part of the story.

The geographic borders of the American South expanded during the antebellum era. The western borders had been continuously contested in the colonial South. The westward migration of European settlements was slow and steady throughout the eighteenth century. For most of the century, Southerners relied on the Indians for survival and to prosper economically. In 1758, over 355,000 pounds of deerskins, brought to the settlers primarily by Indian warriors, left Charles Town harbor for Great Britain. Deerskins also left Savannah, New Orleans, and East and West Florida in slightly smaller quantities. Deerskins remained an important export for the region until the end of the eighteenth century. Georgia was similarly reliant on the Indian warriors.

In the early nineteenth century, cotton offered the ability to end this system of mutual reliance between Indians and settlers. The profitable cultivation of cotton allowed residents in the Lower South to abandon the trade in deerskins which had funded much of their colonial growth. Southerners could afford to remove the southeastern Indians from Georgia, Alabama, Mississippi, Florida, South, Carolina, North Carolina, and Tennessee. In addition, settlers now had sufficient economic reasons to possess former Indian lands. Forced removal of the southeastern Indians to reserved lands in Oklahoma provided hundreds of thousands of fertile acres for Southern planters to plant cotton.

The expansion of African slavery was directly linked with cotton cultivation. Over the course of the first half of the nineteenth century, the future and fortunes of the American South became undeniably tied to the "peculiar institution" of chattel slavery. In the Old South, slavery became more coherent as an institution. African-American slaves struggled to assert cultural autonomy and protect their families in systems that denied their humanity. Southern states passed relatively similar slave codes, and each state formally curtailed the legal rights of blacks—free or slave. Publicly funded slave patrols controlled the Southern countryside, and after the failed Nat Turner Rebellion in 1831 the fear of slave uprisings furthered the need for solidarity among white Southerners. In the political realm, the fear of slave rebellions and the importance of the westward expansion of slavery shaped voting patterns and political affiliations. The political compromises of the early nineteenth century—the Missouri Compromise, the Compromise of 1850, and the Kansas Nebraska-Act—all resulted from the dictates of slavery in antebellum America. The expansion of slavery—in large part due to cotton cultivation—transformed Southern politics and the Southern countryside.

During the early nineteenth century, cotton became king in the American South. Although the entire region did not share in the economic boom equally, the new crop came to symbolize the region in the way that tobacco had earlier defined Virginia and rice had defined South Carolina. Cotton provided the means for the Southern system of slavery to extend westward and for the American South to grow in size and in strength. It was this optimistic American South that would later declare its autonomy from the United States, form the Confederate States of America, and fight the American Civil War.

The Trail of Tears

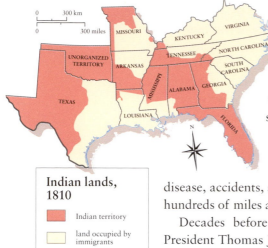

Indian lands, 1810

- Indian territory
- land occupied by immigrants

In the early nineteenth century, tens of thousands of southeastern Indians endured what has been called the "Trail of Tears." Each of the southeastern Indian nations experienced forced removal in this era. Usually on foot, after months of detainment, against their will, and with inadequate resources, food, or medical supplies, Choctaws, Creeks, Chickasaws, Cherokees, and Seminoles were forced off their ancestral lands. In addition to the disruptive aftershocks caused by a forced migration, thousands of native peoples lost their lives to disease, accidents, and malnutrition. Those that survived ended their journey hundreds of miles away in present-day Oklahoma.

Decades before Indian removal became official United States policy, President Thomas Jefferson considered exchanging western lands acquired in the Louisiana Purchase for lands occupied by Natives east of the Mississippi. Although Jefferson did not pursue this plan, subsequent treaties in the first decades of the 1800s encouraged westward removal with financial grants for the affected tribes. The United States officially "reserved" land west of Arkansas in present-day Oklahoma for the southeastern Indians. Hundreds of Natives voluntarily moved west in the early nineteenth century, but most southeastern Indians still remained when the United States elected Andrew Jackson president in 1828.

Jackson's ascendancy to the presidency all but assured a federal policy of forced removal. Jackson, a Southerner from Tennessee, echoed a rationale for removal that was widely shared by his neighbors: "Surrounded by the whites with their arts of civilization, which by destroying the resources of the savage doom him to weakness and decay, the fate of the Mohegan, the Narragansett, and the Delaware is fast overtaking the Choctaws, the Cherokee, and the Creek." Removal, Jackson stated, was the only way for the Indians to avoid their otherwise inevitable destruction. In May 1830, Congress passed the Indian Removal Act which authorized President Jackson to negotiate removal treaties with Indian nations living east of the Mississippi.

The Choctaws were the first to face Jackson's policy of forced removal. In 1830, Jackson arranged the Treaty of Dancing Rabbit Creek to force eastern Choctaws off their land. Over the next three years, groups of Choctaws embarked on a journey that Alexis de Tocqueville described as a "sight [that] will never fade from my memory." The images were chilling. "It was then in the depths of winter, and that year the cold was exceptionally severe; the snow was hard on the ground, and huge masses of ice drifted on the river. The Indians brought their families with them; there were among them the wounded, the sick, newborn babies, and old men on the point of death. They had neither tents nor wagons, but only some provisions and weapons." The term "Trail of Tears" came from the Choctaw's experience in 1831, as entire families and communities died of disease and exposure on the snow-covered trails.

The suffering of the Choctaws was later surpassed by that of the Cherokees. Their removal ensued shortly after the 1828 election of Jackson, when several Cherokees negotiated a removal agreement with the United States. Major Ridge, a Cherokee planter and soldier, and his son John Ridge and nephew Elias Boudinot conducted these negotiations with the United States. Most Cherokees, including Principal Chief John Ross, protested and tried to stop Ridge and his so-called "Treaty Party." Ross hired former attorney general William Wirt to represent the Cherokees in *Cherokee Nation v. Georgia* (1831) and then in *Worcester v. Georgia* (1832). In each case, the Supreme Court recognized the sovereignty of the Cherokee people, and in the latter the Court ruled that the state of Georgia could not make laws for the Cherokee people. Legal victories were not enough to forestall forced removal, as Georgia refused to recognize Cherokee sovereignty. Jackson embraced the Cherokee minority, and together they signed the Treaty of New Echota in 1835. Ridge ceded all Cherokee lands east of the Mississippi in return for lands in present-day northeastern Oklahoma, five million dollars, transportation west, and one year of subsistence. Amid a chorus of protests by Cherokees and their white supporters, the Senate ratified the treaty. Nearly two thousand Cherokees moved west in accordance with the treaty, but most of the nation stayed put. In 1838, the United States army moved in to begin the removal process. After the Cherokees were confined to disease-ridden removal camps for several months, the federal troops forced the Cherokees west. Nearly one quarter of the Cherokee nation died in the camps and on the journeys to reserved lands in Oklahoma.

The other southeastern Indian nations experienced similar stories of upheaval and dislocation. Although each resisted in their own fashion, they too found their ways on the Trail of Tears. Divisions within the Creek Nation led to the execution of William McIntosh, one of its prominent chiefs, for signing the 1825 Treaty of Indian Springs. Despite its continued opposition, the Creek Nation moved west in 1836. Hundreds of Seminoles moved west in 1832, but many more refused to leave the swamps of Florida. Instead, they fought the Second Seminole War (1835-1842) and some remained in the Everglades as the only unconquered Native group in the United States.

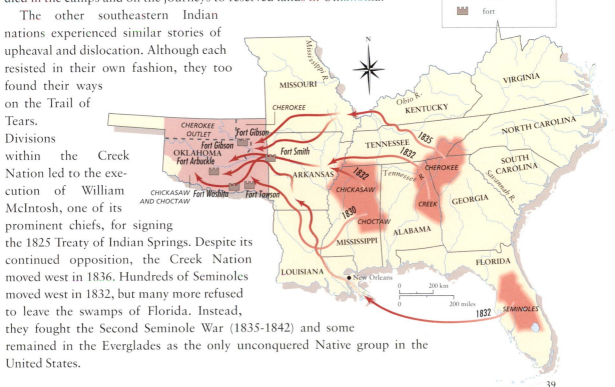

Removal of the Indians, 1829–40

Indian homelands

land reservations west of the Mississippi

1830 primary route taken, with date of most significant removal treaty

fort

The Peculiar Institution

Slaves at work on Pope's plantation, Beaufort County, South Carolina.

In the early nineteenth century, many Americans began to refer to slavery as the South's "peculiar institution." Indeed, a labor system that once spanned the thirteen colonies had become confined solely to the Southern states. One at a time, Northern states passed laws that gradually abolished slavery, and by 1810, slavery was all but banished in the North. The geographic isolation of slavery hardly diminished America's reliance on unfree labor. As Northern masters rid themselves of the institution of slavery, Southern masters expanded their holdings. A nation with 700,000 African-American slaves in 1790 expanded to one with nearly 1.2 million in 1810 and two million in 1830.

The growth of slavery resulted from the new demands of the Industrial Revolution. The emergence of mills in England and New England created heightened demands for raw materials from the South. The demands of the textile mills seemed insatiable. As cotton cultivation moved westward onto vacated Indian lands, slaves performed the backbreaking work required to turn cotton into "white gold." In response to industrial growth, slaves also found their ways into urban and industrial settings. In Southern towns, as well as in the countryside, slaves worked as skilled artisans, blacksmiths, preachers, carpenters, and drivers. Others worked in coal mines, performed industrial labor, and were hired out by their masters on weekly, monthly, and annual contracts. As slavery expanded, it became a flexible labor source.

Most slaves lived on large plantations with a dozen or more other slaves. Large plantations also demanded that slaves perform multiple functions. They tended to every aspect of a wide range of staple products that included cotton, corn, hemp, rice, sugar, and tobacco. Tasks related to crop cultivation consumed most of the year, with the harvest usually demanding the longest and hardest hours. Slaves hoed, weeded, picked, watered, reaped, dried, and planted. Masters even used some slaves to oversee the behavior of their fellow slave laborers. In the slower months, they mended fences, cleared lands, and performed other seasonal tasks. Large plantations also contained house slaves. Although not all domestic tasks were reserved for females, slave women frequently served as nursemaids, child care workers, and cooks for their planter masters. On the large plantations, slaves created vibrant communities in which they formed relatively stable extended families, created Afro-Christian churches, and fostered African-American traditions and customs.

While most slaves lived within a large slave community, most masters owned less than two slaves. In 1860, less than three percent of Southern slaveholders owned more than fifty slaves, and less than 0.1 percent owned more than two hundred slaves. On the typical small farm, African-American slaves and Southern white masters worked alongside each other. In comparison to the larger plantations, there was less division of labor among the slaves on the small farms. Individuals were often fieldhands by day and houseservants by night. Living on small farms proved to be obstacles to the slaves' ability to create families and participate in larger communities.

Most masters were white farmers, but this was not always the case. Native Americans—especially Cherokees, Creeks, and Choctaws—also owned black slaves. After the American Revolution, all of the southeastern Indian nations contained masters and slaves. In each nation, slaveholders represented a small minority of the total population which emulated aspects of Southern white society. As early as 1820, the Cherokees began to copy the slave codes of their neighboring Southern states. Over the next four decades, they pro-hibited intermarriage between slaves and masters and made it unlawful for slaves to own property. These southeastern Indians participated in the internal slave trade, organized patrols to prevent uprisings, and required slaves to carry passes when they traveled. Even some free African-Americans owned slaves of their own. Although this phenomenon was rela-tively rare, 122 free black residents of Charleston, South Carolina owned slaves in 1860. One of them, William Ellison owned sixty-three of his own.

In 1860, just prior to the outbreak of the American Civil War, nearly four million slaves lived in fifteen states. The institution extended west to Texas, south through Florida, and north to Delaware and Maryland. Slavery contin-ued to defy simple characterization, but the connection between the "peculiar institution" and the South was undeniable. Only a bloody war would bring that relationship to an end.

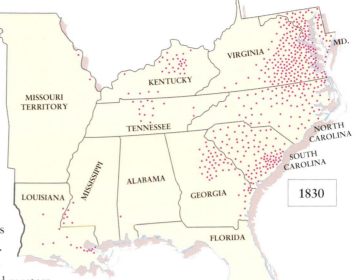

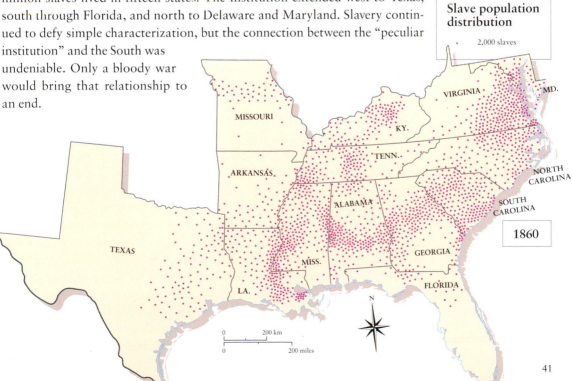

Cotton Becomes King

In 1858, South Carolinian James Henry Hammond boasted that "The slave-holding South is now the controlling power of the world. . . . No power on earth dares . . . to make war on cotton. Cotton is King." On the eve of the Civil War, cotton fields covered nearly the entire region. They swept from North Carolina to Texas and from Tennessee to the Florida panhandle. Only a handful of Upper South states (Virginia, Kentucky, and Missouri) did not reap the financial rewards of the cotton harvest. Eli Whitney's invention of the mechanical cotton gin in 1793 altered the region's agricultural landscape. This new machine swiftly separated the lint from the rough seeds and drastically cut the cost of refining short-staple cotton. Whitney's gin did with ease what otherwise took backbreaking labor. With the accompanying decline in production cost, cotton became the key to the region's economic prosperity.

Planters first grew cotton in the South Carolina and Georgia upcountry. Then they moved it south and west toward occupied Indian lands. With the forced removal of the Creeks, Chickasaws, Choctaws, and Cherokees in the 1830s, the United States made room for the expansion of its Southern cotton kingdom. The 1845 annexation of Texas furthered this spread to the southwest. Cotton created a seemingly insatiable demand. As masters moved west, their slaves and cotton seeds followed. Eventually cotton production became concentrated in what became known as the Cotton Belt, a stretch of fertile land in Alabama, Mississippi, and Louisiana. By the 1830s, these three states grew more than half of the nation's cotton. South Carolina, which grew 60 percent of the crop in 1800, saw its share fall to less than 10 percent on the eve of the Civil War.

The opening of Western lands fostered a complete cotton explosion. Southern states produced a mere three thousand bales in 1790. Twenty years later, they produced over 1.7 million, and on the eve of the Civil War, six million bales. Planters exported most of this cotton, nearly three-quarters, to Great Britain. During the antebellum years, cotton became the nation's leading export in value, exceeding all other American exports combined. Ten percent of all cotton planters produced over half of the cotton crop and the Cotton Belt's wealth. Some planters were, in the words of one Louisianan, "making oceans of money." In 1860, Natchez, Mississippi, had more millionaires per capita than any other town in the nation. One resident, Frederick Stanton, owned 15,000 acres and produced over $122,000 worth of cotton in 1859 alone. The wealth for some led to the despair of others. The success of cotton cultivation resulted in a rise in slave prices, which consequently reinvigorated the domestic, or internal, slave trade. Many slaves from Maryland, Virginia, and the Carolinas found themselves sold and headed toward Georgia, Alabama, Mississippi, Louisiana, and Texas.

Cotton cultivation, however, did not guarantee prosperity. The price of cotton fluctuated wildly during the first half of the nineteenth century. The Panic of 1819 cut the price of cotton nearly in half, and over the next two decades the price continued to vary. Bales that cost 21.5 cents in 1818 and 11.5

cents in 1822 rose in cost slightly in the years that followed. Another economic panic, in 1837, brought the price down further, and cotton plummeted to 5.5 cents in 1844. During the 1850s, cotton's profitability returned. Even as cotton production doubled, heightened demand for the crop kept prices stable. In 1860, cotton hovered at a steady 11 cents.

"King Cotton" did more than rule the Southern economy. Cotton also transformed the Northern states and England. It fueled the Industrial Revolution in both the United States and abroad, and in return, the demand for cotton increased even more. Hundreds of thousands of factory hands relied on the employment that resulted from the South's most plentiful raw material, while millions of others found employment transporting and selling the products. Cotton ensured that for the first half of the nineteenth century, Northerners and Southerners would rely and thrive off one another. Ironically, cotton's close kinship with slavery simultaneously helped make the South culturally distinct from the North.

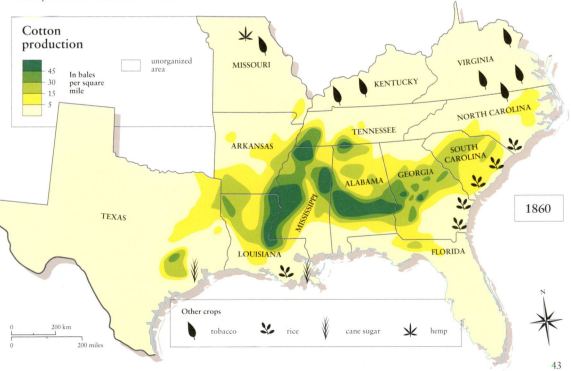

Cotton production

In bales per square mile

- 45
- 30
- 15
- 5

unorganized area

Other crops

tobacco　　rice　　cane sugar　　hemp

1830

1860

0　200 km

0　200 miles

Nat Turner and Antebellum Slave Resistance

"We must and shall be free. . . . And woe, woe, will be it to you if we have to obtain our freedom by fighting. . . . I do declare that one good black man can put to death six white men." With these words, African-American Bostonian David Walker appealed to Southern blacks to rise in violent rebellion. Walker was clear in his meaning. "They want us for their slaves, and think nothing of murdering us in order to subject us to that wretched condition—therefore, if there is an *attempt* by us, kill or be killed. Now, I ask you had you not rather be killed than to be a slave to a tyrant, who takes the life of your mother, wife, and dear little children?" Walker, who was born free in North Carolina, published his *Appeal* in 1829 after generations of American slaves failed to mount coordinated attempts of violent slave resistance.

The American South did not experience anything akin to the 1794 slave rebellion of Toussaint L'Ouverture that resulted in the overthrow of French rule in Saint Domingue and the creation of Haiti. Hundreds of single slaves or small groups of slaves struck at their conditions of bondage violently in the American South, but these acts of rebellion did not threaten the region's system of slavery. Walker boldly expressed the logic for violent resistance against the oppressive labor system, but only five major slave revolts, or conspiracies for massive revolts, can be documented for the entire history of the American South. None of them succeeded, and all were quickly repressed.

The first uprising, the 1739 Stono Rebellion, occurred in colonial South Carolina. Other major conspiracies occurred in the United States. Three never progressed much beyond the planning stages. In the summer of 1800, several slave artisans, inspired by the libertarian and egalitarian rhetoric of the French Revolution, planned an assault on Richmond, Virginia. Gabriel Prosser and other slaves hoped to capture an arsenal, arm themselves, and then kidnap Governor James Monroe. Before Prosser's Rebellion ever began, however, the local militia put an end to it. In the aftermath, twenty of the slave conspirators were executed. The next revolt occured in 1811 in the Louisiana Territory. In 1822, a similar scheme came to an end before the slaves could initiate their violent acts of rebellion in Charleston, South Carolina. Denmark Vesey, himself a carpenter, organized neighboring black artisans into assault teams and hoped to simultaneously attack various targets. By taking guardhouses and the city's arsenal, Vesey believed he would take control of the city. In June, however, the state's militia stopped the revolt just before it began. Thirty-five conspirators were tried and executed, and thirty-seven free blacks were banished from the state.

The only slave revolt that moved beyond the planning stages in the United States took place in Southampton County, Virginia in 1831. Only two years after David Walker published his appeal, Nat Turner and some seventy other slaves confirmed the long-standing fears of the Southern countryside. Wielding pickaxes and strong religious convictions, Turner hoped to reach the county seat miles away. There, in a village named Jerusalem, Turner planned to seize the armory and fulfill his prophetic vision of freedom. On August 21, Turner and five other slaves met on the outskirts of Joseph Travis's plantation. They initiated the attack that evening and began killing white Southerners in the region. The first victim was Travis, Turner's master. From there, the rebels hit neighboring houses. After assaults at a handful of plantations, the rebels reached the Whitehead plantation. There, the escaped slaves killed Margaret Whitehead by "repeated blows with a sword." The rebels continued their reign of terror, and their ranks swelled. By the next day, at least sixty slaves had joined the assault force. On the 23rd, Turner directed the group toward Jerusalem and its arsenal. Along the way, they tried to enlist the help of James Parker's slaves. After unexpected delays at Parker's home, a group of heavily armed white volunteers attacked the rebellious slaves. Turner tried to regroup and enlist more help, but his defeat was all but sealed. On the next morning, American soldiers arrived to put down the rebellion. Turner escaped the initial attempts at his capture by hiding in the woods near several plantations, but most of his fellow conspirators were quickly killed or captured. In the two months that it took to apprehend Turner, Virginians executed twenty slaves and evicted ten others out of the state. On November 11, merely twelve days after his capture, Turner was hanged. The most "successful" slave revolt had come to a deadly close.

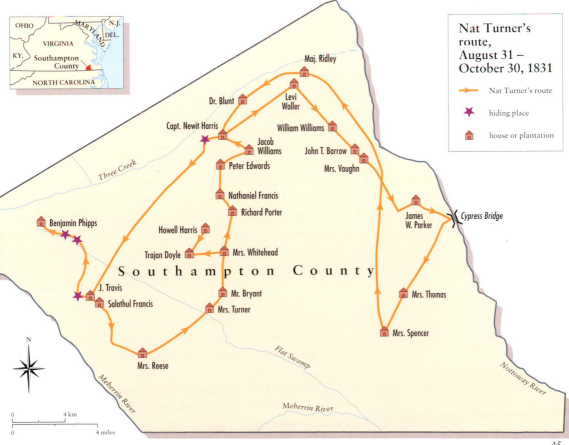

Nat Turner's route, August 31 – October 30, 1831

→ Nat Turner's route

★ hiding place

⌂ house or plantation

Underground Railroad and Paths to Freedom

Harriet Tubman helped perhaps three hundred slaves to escape to the North.

In 1849, Harriet Tubman walked from slavery to freedom. "Liberty or death" Tubman recalled. "If I could not have one, I would have the other." Convinced that she was about to be sold, Tubman ran away from Maryland by following the brooks and streams to Philadelphia and freedom. Tubman also used the assistance of white and black antislavery sympathizers to find her way to Philadelphia. In the following years, Tubman returned to the South nineteen times to escort other African-Americans away from the "peculiar institution" and toward the "Promised Land" of the North. Stopping at prearranged "stations" along the way, Tubman was personally responsible for freeing some three hundred African-Americans, including her aging parents and siblings. Tubman's fame as a "conductor" on the "Underground Railroad" attracted the ire of many white Southerners, and there was a $40,000 bounty for her capture. At the same time, her many supporters proclaimed her to be the "Moses of her People."

The Underground Railroad that Tubman participated in was a loosely defined network of whites and blacks who provided assistance and shelter to fugitive slaves. Aiding fugitives was punishable in all of the Southern states, and expressions of antislavery sentiment in the South was paramount to treason. The passage of the federal Fugitive Slave Act in 1850 made assisting runaways punishable in the North as well. Participants frequently ended their involvement as a result of paranoia; even so, the fears that their actions were being watched were not always unfounded. White and black Southerners frequently betrayed the Underground Railroad by leading runaways into the hands of law officers and slave catchers. Tubman recognized the dangers of such a system and tried to follow different paths on each of her journeys. Most escaped slaves remained in the United States, but some found freedom in Canada, where the British government refused to extradite slaves.

Fugitive slaves usually acted as individuals rather than as part of an organized system. Often under the cover of darkness, runaways employed as many means of transportation as they could. Generally, walking was the only option. These acts were often no less brazen than those associated with the Underground Railroad. In perhaps the most imaginative escape, Henry "Box" Brown nailed himself inside a wooden crate and had himself shipped from Richmond to Philadelphia. He lined the box—which measured 2 feet 8 inches deep, 2 feet wide, and 3 feet long—with baize and filled it with a handful of biscuits and some water. The box—marked "This side up with care"—brought Brown safely out of slavery. Frederick Douglass employed a much more common method to escape bondage in Baltimore, Maryland. He boarded a Delaware bound train with identification papers he borrowed from a free black sailor. From Wilmington, he took a boat to Philadelphia. Other runaways obtained the assistance of white "conductors," who posed as gentlemen at railroad stations until they met up with a runaway slave. Then the two traveled north together, with the slave posing as a manservant for the duration of the trip.

Many escaped slaves chose to stay in the American South, often hiding within miles of their former plantation. These runaways usually remained near their still-enslaved families. Reuniting families, especially after the auction block separated husbands from wives and children, became a powerful motive for running away. Other runaway slaves formed maroon communities on the frontier. Distant and inhospitable environments, like the Great Dismal Swamp in North Carolina and Virginia, attracted large communities of runaway slaves. Other fugitives, especially those from the Lower South, found refuge among southeastern Indians. The Seminoles, for example, provided freedom to several hundred African-Americans; the marshes of the neighboring Everglades hid hundreds more. However, escape from white slaveowners to neighboring Indians did not necessarily mean freedom. Hundreds of slaves escaped to the southeastern Indians only to be sold back into slavery or held as bondsmen by the Indians themselves.

Close to one thousand slaves—mostly from the Upper South—successfully escaped slavery in the antebellum South each year. The fate of runaways were not always secure after the journey from slavery to freedom ended, but the lure of freedom was a great motivator for many. Despite the courage of Tubman and thousands of other fugitive slaves, however, most slaves never took to the road. The risks were too great and the opportunities too limited. Slaves would not walk from slavery to freedom en masse until Union lines penetrated the Southern countryside during the American Civil War.

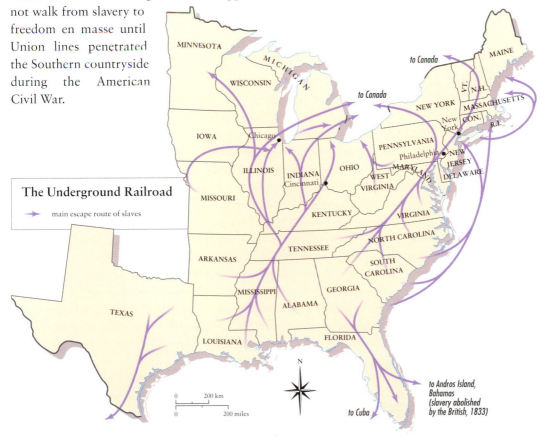

The Underground Railroad

→ main escape route of slaves

The Battle over the West

Missouri compromise, 1820

☐ Louisiana Purchase, 1803

▓ free state / territory, 1820   ▓ slave state / territory, 1820

When President Thomas Jefferson arranged the Louisiana Purchase in 1803, he added 828,000 square miles to the United States and provided the young republic with what seemed to be limitless lands. Kentucky and Tennessee had been recently admitted as slave states in 1792 and 1796, and the Mississippi Territory offered some room for expansion. Even so, the Louisiana Purchase provided room for national growth on an unprecedented scale. The boundless lands of the West seemed to be a solution to the nation's most pressing economic and political problems. For many white Southerners, the new lands provided a means to expand cotton planting and slaveholding.

The new territory did not prove to be the immediate panacea that Jefferson and others had foreseen. Although the newly acquired Western lands provided independence and prosperity for some, they also became the nation's battleground over slavery and its expansion. When the admission of Missouri came to the floor of the House of Representatives in 1819, the battle over slavery reared its ugly head. As Jefferson wrote at the time, the Missouri issue "like a fire-bell in the night, awakened and filled me with terror." Slavery was well entrenched in the territory, existing in the region long before the Louisiana

Purchase ended decades of Spanish and French rule. Still, New York Congressman James Tallmadge led the fight against admitting Missouri as a slave state. He introduced an amendment to the bill for Missouri statehood that prohibited the future importation of slaves into Missouri and gradually emancipated the slaves already in the territory. After a bitter debate, the House passed the Tallmadge Amendment in a strictly sectional vote. The Senate was not as quick to ratify it, however, and Missouri remained a territory when the Fifteenth Congress adjourned. Internal dissent prevented the Senate from taking action once again when Congress reconvened for the Sixteenth Congress. The "Great Compromiser," Senator Henry Clay of Kentucky, finally pushed a series of agreements through the Senate in the Seventeenth Congress. That Missouri Compromise stated that Missouri would be admitted as a slave state, while Maine would enter as a free state. This would preserve the balance of power between North and South in the Senate. In addition, Congress drew a free-slave line through the territories at Missouri's southern border, 36° 30'. Territory to the north would be free and that to the south, slave.

The issue of statehood for the other Western territories, Clay hoped, would not evoke these divisive debates again. Until 1850, Clay's Missouri Compromise worked rather well. Arkansas, Florida, and Texas were admitted as slave states while Iowa, Wisconsin, and Michigan became free states. Clay's plan allowed the United States to incorporate new states without disturbing the sectional balance in the Senate, as each new slave state was accompanied by a free state. As 1850 approached, however, the Missouri Compromise would

Slave quarters on a small plantation in Georgia.

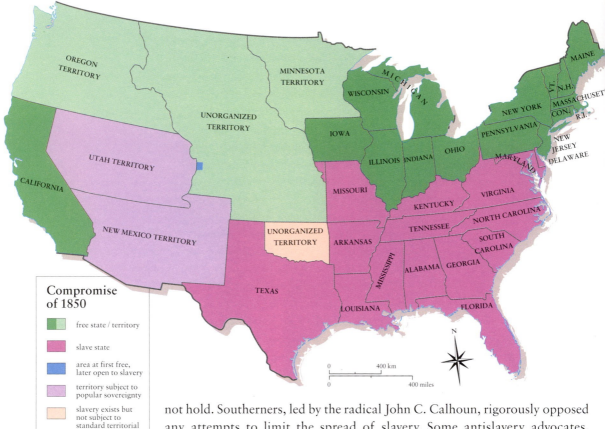

Compromise of 1850

- ■ free state / territory
- ■ slave state
- ■ area at first free, later open to slavery
- ■ territory subject to popular sovereignty
- ■ slavery exists but not subject to standard territorial sovereignty

not hold. Southerners, led by the radical John C. Calhoun, rigorously opposed any attempts to limit the spread of slavery. Some antislavery advocates, including William H. Seward and Salmon P. Chase, opposed any expansion of slavery with equal ferocity. When California, New Mexico, and Utah applied for statehood, few thought that the law of 36° 30' would hold. It pleased neither extreme.

Black population in the United States, 1800–60: Total number and proportion of total population

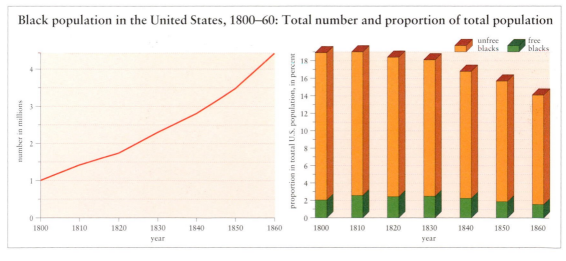

The ensuing compromise took several months of negotiations before it was passed by Congress. Once again a series of bills addressed the issue. Orchestrated by Clay, Daniel Webster, and Stephen A. Douglas, the Compromise of 1850 established California as a free state and left the futures of New Mexico and Utah in the hands of popular sovereignty. Each territory would hold elections and determine its future concerning slavery before applying for statehood. The compromise addressed other sectional issues as well. Congress strengthened the Fugitive Slave Act by requiring federal officials to return runaway slaves. In return, the internal slave trade was abolished in Washington, DC. This compromise averted a sectional crisis and brought three new states into the union. However, it outraged many Northerners and Southerners. As soon as it was signed, dissenters avowed that they would fight the laws.

Rather than solving the nation's problems, the Western Territories exacerbated national tensions. As territorial lands approached statehood, they threatened the precarious sectional balance and the Union itself. The question of slavery took on symbolic importance in the West, as Southerners and Northerners alike knew that the decisions there would determine the future of the nation. The political compromises that addressed this issue temporarily preserved the free-slave balance in the United States Senate, but they could not mend the growing anxieties between the regions themselves. After the 1850s, these sectional tensions escaped the political venues of debate and rhetoric and manifested themselves as physical violence.

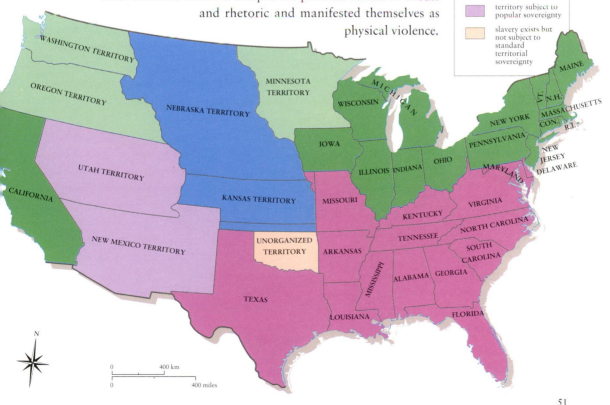

Kansas-Nebraska Act, 1854

- free state / territory
- slave state
- area at first free, later open to slavery
- territory subject to popular sovereignty
- slavery exists but not subject to standard territorial sovereignty

Bleeding Kansas and John Brown

The concept of popular sovereignty had its biggest test in the Kansas Territory. Four years after the Compromise of 1850, the future of the Kansas Territory came to Congress. At first, it appeared that another compromise would win the day. The Kansas-Nebraska Act split the Kansas territory into two states, both of whose destinies would be determined by popular sovereignty and the ballot box. Although the elections were held locally, voters came to Kansas from across the nation. Thousands of settlers—slaveholders and abolitionists—rushed to Kansas in order to cast their vote and shape the nation's future. Missouri Senator David R. Atchinson led hundreds of proslavery residents across state lines and to the Kansas polls. William H. Seward similarly urged Northerners west. "Come on then, Gentlemen of the Slave States," he urged, "since there is no escaping your challenge, I accept it in behalf of the cause of freedom. We will engage in competition for the virgin soil of Kansas, and God give the victory to the side which is stronger in numbers as it is in right."

Supported by the New England Emigrant Aid Society, hundreds of abolitionists traveled to and voted in Kansas. Both abolitionists and slaveholders saw Kansas as a place for the spread of their regional cultures and values. More importantly, they understood the political implications that a free or slave Kansas might have on the nation at large. In the months that followed, slavery proponents and opponents held competing state constitutional conventions, won separate elections, and organized dueling governments in Kansas. When United States President Franklin Pierce recognized the proslavery legislature in Lecompten, the free-soilers refused to recognize its legitimacy. Kansan polarization quickly turned into violence and guerrilla warfare. In May 1856, some 700 proslavery men sacked Lawrence, Kansas, looting and destroying free-soil newspaper offices, stores, and buildings. In the end, violence proliferated throughout the state.

The blood shed over popular sovereignty was not confined to the territories. The violence over slavery extended to Congress. On May 21, 1856, South Carolina Congressman Preston Brooks entered the United States Senate and approached an aged senator from Massachusetts, Charles Sumner. In the minutes that followed, Brooks verbally berated the elder statesman and then proceeded to strike him over his head with a gutta-percha cane. The assault continued even after a handful of blows broke the cane. When the beating ended, Sumner and the cane lay bloodied and broken on the Senate floor. The dispute over Kansas formed the base of the personal antagonism between Brooks and Sumner. Two

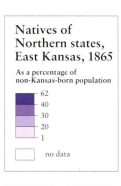

Natives of Northern states, East Kansas, 1865

As a percentage of non-Kansas-born population

- 62
- 40
- 30
- 20
- 1

no data

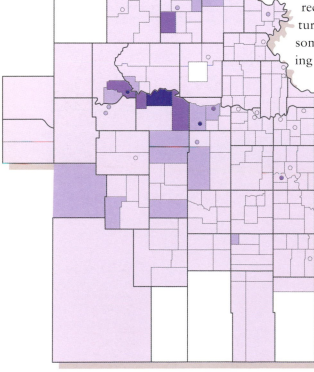

days earlier, Sumner, a long-time abolitionist, issued a fiery "Crime Against Kansas" speech. This powerful oration outlined more than the illegitimacy of the Lecompten legislature, the actions of the Pierce administration, and the basic tenets of the abolition movement. Sumner also chastised the proslavery "thugs" from South Carolina, depicted "the drunken spew and vomit of an uneasy civilization," and denounced Andrew P. Butler as a "Don Quixote who had chose a mistress to whom he has made his vows, . . . the harlot, Slavery." For Brooks, the younger nephew and protégé of Butler, these insults demanded a violent answer. Although Sumner and other Northerners saw the caning as nothing less than a sign of Southern barbarity, Southerners proclaimed Brooks to be a regional hero. The beaten Sumner did not return to the Senate floor for over two years, and for many his empty seat symbolized the virtue of the abolitionist cause and the savagery of slaveholding. Brooks returned to South Carolina, where he was reelected and presented with several commemorative canes.

John Brown, a northern-born abolitionist, was especially horrified by Brooks's actions. The day after the caning of Sumner, Brown avenged the attacks on Lawrence, Kansas, and on Sumner in Pottawatomie Creek, Kansas. Armed with razor-sharp broadswords, Brown, four of his sons, a son-in-law, and two others, proclaimed themselves to be the "Army of the North." Late that evening, they forced themselves into the cabins of three proslavery families. By the time the Pottawatomie Massacre had ended, Brown and his men had split the skulls or otherwise mutilated five men. In October 1859, Brown led yet another assault on what he saw as an evil "Slave Power." With the financial backing of several abolitionist supporters in Boston, Brown led a heavily armed assault team of eighteen and seized the federal arsenal at Harpers Ferry, Virginia. He planned to provide enough guns for a slave rebellion that would finally put an end to slavery and create a black republic in the South. Colonel Robert E. Lee quickly ended the attack. Brown was captured and ten of his men were killed. Brown was charged with treason and sentenced to death on November 2, 1859. During the one month that passed before his execution, Brown offered himself as a martyr to the cause of antislavery. Minutes before he hanged, Brown handed a prophetic note to his jailer that read "I John Brown am now quite certain that the crimes of this guilty land will never be purged away; but with blood."

Natives of South-Midland states, East Kansas, 1865

As a percentage of non-Kansas-born population

- 77
- 40
- 30
- 20
- 4

no data

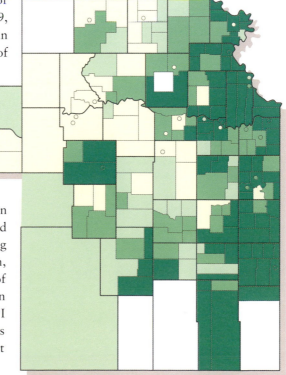

Democratic Divisions

On April 23, 1860, the Democratic Party's national convention convened in Charleston, South Carolina. Recent events—including John Brown's raid at Harpers Ferry, the Supreme Court's Dred Scott ruling, and the ever-increasing power of the Republican Party—led to a tense atmosphere. The question of slavery in the West threatened to tear apart the Democratic Party—the only political party with national support.

The convention was held in the heart of proslavery radicalism, several blocks from John C. Calhoun's grave. This location only added fuel to the sectional fires. Sectional rhetoric and ambitions divided the convention, and emotions flared at a feverish pitch. The proslavery radicals, encouraged by cheering crowds, were determined to prevent front-runner Stephen A. Douglas from obtaining the party's nomination. His support for popular sovereignty and his refusal to protect the expansion of slavery was unacceptable. Robert Barnwell Rhett's *Charleston Mercury* condemned any compromise with the Douglas forces, and the "Southern rights" speeches and meetings aroused the passions of hundreds of participants in the days before the convention. Southern representatives demanded a party platform that guaranteed the federal protection of slavery in the territories. They would not compromise on this count—the stakes were too high. In response to calls for moderation, Alabama fire-eater William Lowndes Yancey told a chorus of cheers that "Ours are the institutions which are at stake; ours is the property that is to be destroyed; ours is the honor at stake." Douglas felt he had no choice but to oppose directly these sentiments and reject the proslavery proposal. When the regional confrontation became too heated and a two-thirds

Presidential election, 1852

- Pierce (Democrat)
- Hale (Free-Soil Democrat)
- Scott (Whig)
- Webster (Independent Whig)
- Troup (Southern Rights Party)
- no return

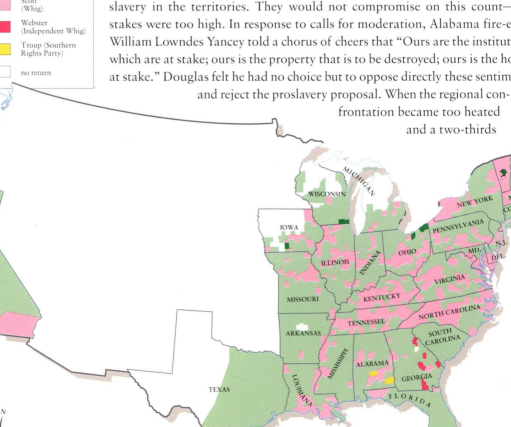

N

0   300 km

0   300 miles

majority could not concur on a nomination, the delegates from the Lower South and Arkansas stormed out of the convention. The representatives adjourned with a plan to reconvene six weeks later in Baltimore, Maryland.

June in Baltimore proved no cure for the sectional divisions. Symbolically, Baltimore was more hospitable to the competing factions because it was the geographic middle ground between the North and South. In addition, Baltimore did not have the same emotionally charged atmosphere as did Charleston. However, the political divisions within the Democratic Party did not disappear in this new setting. The convention reconvened but did not move ahead. Once again, the party split along regional lines. These irreconcilable differences became more pronounced when the Douglas forces continued with the nomination process while the Southern delegates met at another Baltimore hall the next day. The Democratic Party now contained separate Northern and Southern entities that nominated separate party tickets and wrote separate policy platforms. Northerners and Westerners nominated Douglas as their presidential candidate with Benjamin Fitzpatrick of Alabama as vice president, and adopted a platform that included a policy of congressional noninterference in the territories. When Fitzpatrick decided not to run, Herschel V. Johnson of Georgia took his place on the ticket. The separate Southern Democratic Convention overwhelmingly gave its support to current Vice President John C. Breckinridge of Kentucky for President and Oregon Senator Joseph Lane as his running mate. Their platform included a federal slave code for the territories.

Harpers Ferry engine house, where the slave rebellion led by John Brown took place.

The breakup of the only cross-regional political party encouraged some former Whigs, Know-Nothings, and other dissatisfied men to form the Constitutional Union party in 1860. This new party also convened in Baltimore, where members tried to create a national voting base. Delegates called for universal allegiance to the Constitution and proclaimed that patriotism and stability were their unifying motives. They nominated former Whigs to the Presidential ticket—John Bell of Tennessee and Edward Everett of Massachusetts as his running mate.

The election of 1860 was contested by four political parties. The Constitutional Union Party carried the 39 electoral votes of Kentucky, Tennessee and Virginia, but could attract only 12.6 percent of the national vote. The Northern Democrat Douglas received support from all of the states

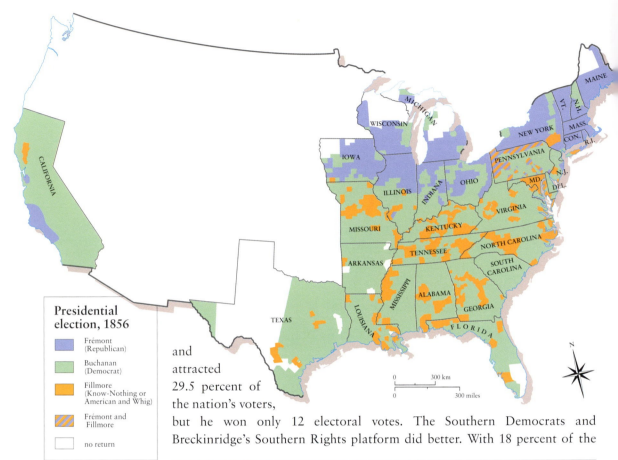

Presidential election, 1856

- ▩ Frémont (Republican)
- ▩ Buchanan (Democrat)
- ▩ Fillmore (Know-Nothing or American and Whig)
- ▩ Frémont and Fillmore
- ☐ no return

and attracted 29.5 percent of the nation's voters, but he won only 12 electoral votes. The Southern Democrats and Breckinridge's Southern Rights platform did better. With 18 percent of the

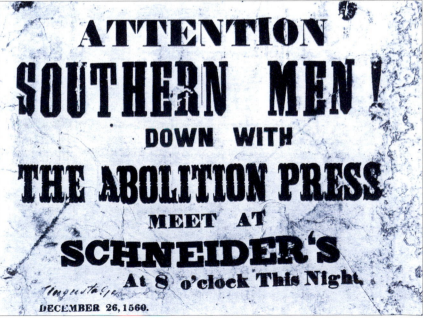

A quickly printed hand bill advertising a pro-slavery meeting.

A 1860 cartoon shows Breckinridge (middle) tearing off the South while Lincoln and Douglas (left) are busy fighting for control elsewhere. Standing on a chair with a small brush and a little glue, Bell (right) does not look as if he could put the country back together.

popular vote, he won 72 electoral seats. Even so, combined, these three candidates did not have enough electoral votes to defeat Abraham Lincoln, the Republican Party nominee. Because of the anti-slavery sentiments within his party, Lincoln's name did not even appear on the ballot in ten slave states. Nevertheless, he received 39.8 percent of the nation's vote and won the presidency with 180 electoral votes.

Presidential election, 1860

- Lincoln (Republican)
- Douglas (Democrat)
- Breckinridge (Democrat)
- Bell (Constitutional Union)
- divided
- no return

PART III: THE CONFEDERATE SOUTH

The American Civil War was a defining moment in the American South. The creation of the Confederate States of America turned a geographic expression with ambiguous borders into a cohesive and self-conscious nation. Even before the war began, secession demanded a regional unity that had not previously existed. In 1861, it became clear that the eleven seceded states comprised the cultural area of the American South. At the same time, those slave states that remained in the Union divorced themselves from the region. The Confederacy institutionalized more than a sense of geographic certainty for the region. It also created a Southern capital, Southern currency, Southern constitution, Southern government, Southern president and cabinet, Southern armed forces, and Southern nationality. Although these wartime creations had their fates tied to the battlefield, other creations of the Confederacy did not. For many Southerners, the Confederacy confirmed or created a regional civilization that would be celebrated for generations to follow. The war provided a cast of regional heroes such as Robert E. Lee and Stonewall Jackson, and another cast of villains such as William Tecumseh Sherman and Philip Sheridan. It also provided a catalogue of symbols and ideologies; the Confederate battle flag, for example, has maintained powerful regional identifications ever since the end of the war. The war also created over 250,000 Southern-born martyrs to the Confederate cause, thousands of memorials and graveyards, and countless stories of individual courage and struggles of despair.

During the American Civil War, Confederate nationalism united many white Southerners in ways that they had never been unified before. In the aftermath of Abraham Lincoln's 1860 election, Southern nationalists organized parades and urged their neighbors to unite behind the Confederate banner. The Civil War allowed the South, in the words of Southern journalist Wilbur J. Cash, to reach maturity. "Four years of fighting," he wrote "left these Southerners far more self-conscious than they had been before, far more aware of their differences and of the line which divided what was Southern from what was not." Even as Union troops occupied Confederate lands, many Southerners continued to echo this sense of regional solidarity. One woman in Milledgeville, Georgia, did not lose hope when her city fell into the hands of Union troops. "The yankee flag waved from the Capitol—Our degradation was bitter, but we knew it could not be long, and we never desponded, our trust was still strong. No, we went through the house singing, 'We live and die with [Confederate President Jefferson] Davis.' How can they hope to subjugate the South? The people are firmer than ever before." Confederate nationalism did not survive the war completely, but the memories of a unified and defiant American South persisted for generations after the war ended.

The four-year war did not merely have regional importance. In many ways, the American Civil War transformed the United States. Over 620,000 soldiers—two percent of all Americans alive in 1860—died as a result of the war. Many more were wounded, and frequently soldiers received wounds on separate occasions. Some American communities buried an entire generation of

Richmond, Virginia, shown here, like many cities in the South, suffered the ravages of bombardment, fire, and occupation.

their young men during the course of the war, while other communities struggled to deal with the soldiers who returned home with mental and physical scars. Few American families escaped the agony of losing kinsmen. For "the generation" that survived, the war left an indelible mark. Supreme Court Justice Oliver Wendell Holmes believed that the Civil War generation "has been set apart by its experience. Through our great good fortune, in our youth our hearts were touched by fire. It was given to us to learn at the outset that life is a profound and passionate thing." Not all Americans looked so longingly upon their war experiences, but few doubted the importance the war had on the soldiers', and the nation's, character.

The war also extracted a heavy cost in money and machinery. Sherman's and Sheridan's raids had devastated the Southern countryside. They destroyed railroads and factories and burned cities and towns. The region's cotton fields would have to wait at least a year before they could be replanted. Homes needed to be rebuilt, and the bridges that were not completely destroyed needed to be mended. Lands where cattle formerly grazed contained neither fences nor animals in the war's aftermath. The emancipation of the region's four hundred thousand African-American slaves also altered the region's economic and social structure. The Confederate dollar became worthless overnight, and most loans made to the Confederacy went unpaid. Confederate General Braxton Bragg returned to his Alabama home after the war only to discover that "*all, all* was lost, except my debts."

The Northern states did not escape the Civil War untouched either. Although their home front did not suffer in the same manner as that of the Confederacy, some of their backyards were turned into battlefields and destroyed. In addition, the financial costs of maintaining the Union army, in terms of salary and machinery, forced the United States to create a paper currency and amass an enormous national debt. The federal budget before the secession crisis had been $63 million, and by 1865 the annual expenditures of the nation were well over one billion dollars. Unlike the devastation in the South, however, the increased federal spending in the North created a financial windfall.

The American Civil War also ended several of the sectional disputes that resulted in warfare. First and foremost, the war ended the battle over African slavery. For generations, abolitionists and slave owners debated the morality, economic necessity, and justification of owning slaves. African-Americans, for their part, had protested the evils of the peculiar institution since its outset. The war put to rest these disputes by providing freedom to the nation's enslaved population and by establishing free labor as the national norm. In 1858, a prophetic Abraham Lincoln declared that "A nation divided against itself cannot survive. I believe this government cannot endure, permanently half slave and half free." The American Civil War ended this sectional division, and the struggle to define "free" dominated the nation's history for the next century.

The American Civil War addressed sectional issues other than slavery. The war also redefined the relationship between the nation and the state. The right of individual states to reject their membership within the Union was formally rejected during the war. The United States never accepted the eleven states that had seceded from the United States; they were instead treated as rebellious. Lincoln's wartime policy emphatically rejected the idea that the Union was comprised of voluntary and sovereign members; the nation was undeniably a single entity with subdivisions called states. The Union victory confirmed this stance. Even the term "The United States" underwent a transition after the war. Before the war began, most Americans believed it to be a plural noun; afterwards, it became singular.

Third, the American Civil War brought the federal government into the daily lives of most Americans for the first time. Most government functions remained controlled on the local level, but the federal government after the war touched aspects of American society that it never approached before. The war centralized the military, created national taxes, initiated the military draft, printed paper money, established a national banking system, and provided the federal government new powers through the Thirteenth through Fifteenth Amendments. When the war ended, the federal government, with

53,000 employees on its payroll, became the nation's largest employer. The largest group of these new employees was responsible for levying and collecting taxes.

The American Civil War was a regional and national event of immense significance. It shaped the history of the American South for the next century, and it forever restructured the United States. Sectionalism did not disappear in the aftermath of the nation's greatest sectional crisis, but the nature of sectionalism forever changed.

A group of Confederate volunteers. Their commitment to the new Confederacy and a belief in their way of life constituted the main strength of the Southern armies.

The Secession Conventions

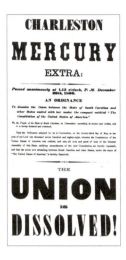

On December 20, 1860, the Charleston Mercury *managed to publish a special edition within minutes of the vote of the Ordinance of Secession.*

On November 7, 1860, news of Abraham Lincoln's presidential victory spread across the nation. As the Republican Party's candidate, Lincoln campaigned solely in Northern states and publicly proclaimed the immorality of slavery. In two months, he would be inaugurated as the sixteenth President of the United States. Inflamed by the election of a man they believed to be an abolitionist, South Carolinians immediately called for a January 8 election of delegates to a secession convention. There, they would formally sever their ties to the Union. The two-month delay between the election and the secession convention, South Carolinians hoped, would provide sufficient time for other Southern states to follow a similar path toward disunion. Ensuing secession rallies in Alabama and Mississippi convinced the South Carolina legislature that two months was too long a delay. It slated December 17, 1860 as the new date for a secession convention. Within a month, Alabama, Florida, Georgia, Louisiana, and Mississippi all planned similar meetings. On December 20, after two days of fiery speeches, the South Carolina delegates officially and unanimously voted to secede from the United States.

In the following month and a half, voters met throughout the Lower South and discussed the futures of their states. By February 1, Louisiana, Mississippi, Alabama, Georgia, Texas, and Florida had joined South Carolina and declared themselves separate from the United States. These states established a provisional Confederate capital in Montgomery, Alabama, and actively campaigned to convince other slaves states to join them. These undecided Upper South states contained a majority of the South's population, food supply, and industrial resources. In essence, they were the key to creating a viable Confederate Nation. In the meantime, the seceded states drafted a provisional Confederate Constitution, and inaugurated Jefferson Davis their President and

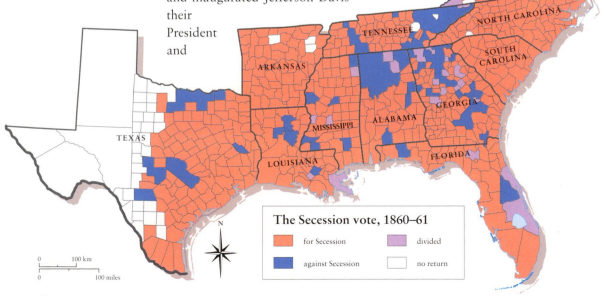

The Secession vote, 1860–61

- for Secession
- against Secession
- divided
- no return

0   100 km

0   100 miles

Alexander H. Stevens their Vice-President. They also began to seize United States forts, post offices, arsenals, customs offices, and other federal property in the region. During his inauguration on March 4, 1861, Lincoln pledged that he would hold on to all of the property that the United States controlled in the seceded states. The United States, however, controlled only four military posts. Three of these forts were in the relatively underpopulated Florida.

The fourth fort remained under the control of federal soldiers even though it was nestled in Charleston Harbor. This control became tenuous as Confederate forces placed Fort Sumter under a blockade. A wary Lincoln knew that the fort would fall if it could not be supplied with basic provisions, but he was determined not to initiate hostilities or to back down. Lincoln's decision to provide provisions, not arms or men, forced the Confederates to escalate the dispute. After informing South Carolina Governor Francis W. Pickens that the supplies were primarily foodstuffs, Lincoln ordered that the fort be resupplied. Negotiations for a peaceful resolution fell through, and Confederate General P. G.T. Beauregard began shelling the island fortress on April 12. After thirty-three hours, the cannons stopped. United States Major Robert Anderson surrendered, and the Confederate flag flew over the ruins of the fort. The Civil War had begun.

Lincoln's decision to confront the blockade forced Southerners to take the first shots of the war. The Union defeat at Sumter allowed him to take more definitive actions against the new Southern nation. After the battle over Fort Sumter, Lincoln declared a national emergency that was "too powerful to be suppressed" by normal means. This enabled him to call for 75,000 volunteers to restore order. Under the terms of enlistment, these soldiers would serve sixty days. The battle at Sumter also forced decisions by slave states in the Upper South and border States. These slave states could no longer maintain their neutrality or wait for a peaceful solution. The outbreak of war mandated that they choose their allegiance, and Virginia, Arkansas, Tennessee, and North Carolina opted to secede from the Union and join the Confederacy. By June 8, 1861, a total of eleven states united under the banner of the Confederate States of America. They moved their capital to Richmond, Virginia, wrote a permanent constitution, and formally elected President Davis. The division between North and South was not simply caused by slavery, however this seemed the most visibly divisive problem. Although all Confederate States contained slaves, other slaveholding states— Maryland, Delaware, Kentucky, and Missouri—remained loyal to the Union. With the geographical lines between North and South rewritten, the bloodiest war in American history began.

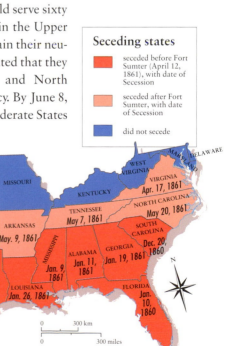

Seceding states

■ seceded before Fort Sumter (April 12, 1861), with date of Secession

■ seceded after Fort Sumter, with date of Secession

■ did not secede

An Unequal Divide

If nations won wars only as a result of material resources and size of armies, then the Civil War would have ended as a quick rout for the Union. When the war began, the North had substantial advantages in both men and machinery. The United States contained over three times as many white men as did the Confederate States of America. Adding to the Union's advantage, close to ninety percent of the nation's industrial capacity existed north of the Mason-Dixon line. The North had eleven times more ships and boats and contained twenty-four times more locomotives than did the Confederacy. The North had twice as many horses and mules, and produced fifteen times more iron, seventeen times more textile goods, and thirty-two times more firearms than the Southern states. Perhaps most important, the North contained about two thirds of the nation's railroad mileage. With less railroad mileage and factories than the Union, the South could easily lose its rail transportation. This was exacerbated by the South's inability to replace

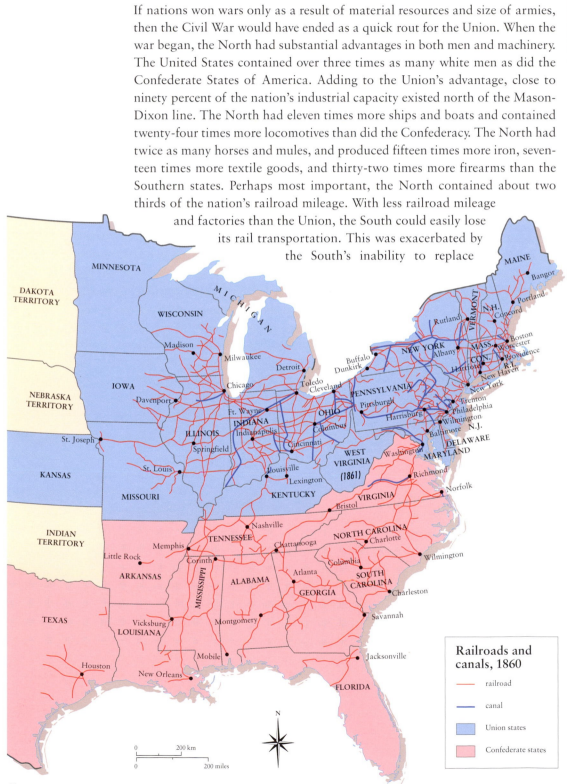

Railroads and canals, 1860

— railroad

— canal

Union states

Confederate states

broken rails. On the human front, Confederate soldiers often went shoeless and had less-than-sufficient daily rations that consisted of little more than bacon, cornmeal, and an occasional handful of rice or black-eyed peas. Despite these Confederate shortcomings, the war lasted for four long years. The Confederacy did not bow down to its statistical inferiority.

The demographic imbalance between North and South naturally led to a drastic inbalance in the armies. An estimated 2.1 million men (half of the eligible men) fought for the Union, while only 850,000 (at least three quarters of those of military age) enlisted in the Confederate forces. Even though Northern casualties and deaths outnumbered Southern ones, the South suffered disproportionately. Nearly one in three Confederate soldiers died during the war, and an additional one in two returned with serious injuries. Conversely, one in six Union soldiers died and one in five were seriously injured. The 3.5 million African-

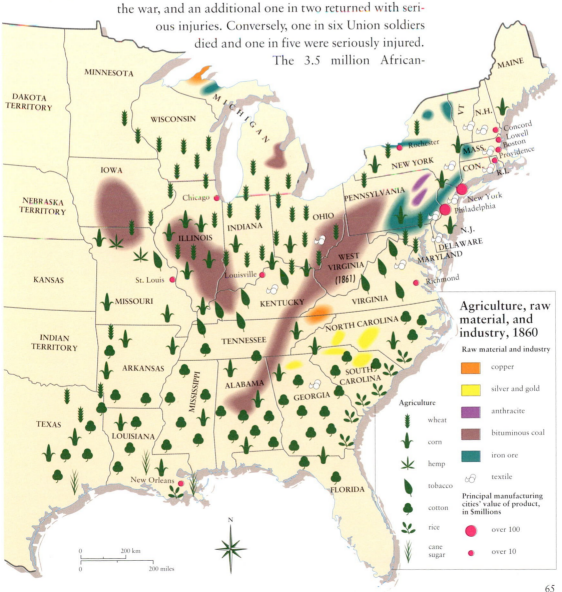

Agriculture, raw material, and industry, 1860

Raw material and industry

- copper
- silver and gold
- anthracite
- bituminous coal
- iron ore
- textile

Agriculture

- wheat
- corn
- hemp
- tobacco
- cotton
- rice
- cane sugar

Principal manufacturing cities' value of product, in $millions

- over 100
- over 10

Colonel Robert E. Lee and General Stonewall Jackson (above) were two popular and capable leaders of an enthusiastic, though poorly equipped, Confederate army (right).

Americans who lived in Southern bondage proved a double-edged sword for the Confederacy. During the Civil War, slaves performed many useful home-front tasks, from tending crops to digging trenches. Blacks never fought for the Confederacy—although this was discussed—but their labor theoretically freed white Confederates for front-line military service. At the same time, the institution of slavery drew resources away from the front lines, as many owners recognized the need to closely watch their slaves. A Confederate conscription law passed in October 1862 exempted a white master on plantations with twenty or more slaves. This reduced the manpower available to the Southern forces. African-American slaves found their own ways to undermine the Confederate cause. They often sabotaged farm tools as well as industrial products, and betrayed the interests of their masters. Slaves also ran to Union lines when possible, and when allowed to do so in 1862, formally enlisted to help the Union fight for their freedom. Nearly 190,000 African-Americans, many of whom had been recently enslaved, fought in the Union army and navy. Abraham Lincoln attested to the importance of the participation of black soldiers in 1864. "We can not spare the hundred and forty or fifty thousand now serving us as soldiers, seamen, and laborers," he insisted. "This is not a question of sentiment or taste, but one of physical force which may be measured and estimated as horse-power and steam-power are measured and estimated. Keep it and you can save the Union. Throw it away, and the Union goes with it."

Rather than accept defeat as a result of its weaknesses, the South adjusted to its demographic realities. The South took measures to bolster its fighting force and make the best use of its natural and industrial resources. The first step in this process included conscripting a wide range of white men. In April 1862, the Confederacy responded to General Robert E. Lee's pleas and began drafting able-bodied white men between the age of eighteen and thirty-five. Five months later, the draft was extended to those men between the ages of seventeen and forty-five. In February 1864, the draft was further expanded to include men under the age of fifty. In another move to preserve Southern independence, the Confederacy restructured its economy to suit its military needs. The Tredegar Iron Works, in Richmond, Virginia, became an important industrial center for the Confederate States of America as it provided needed materials for the war effort. The South produced its own artillery during the war, but even so, it could not keep pace with the Union. Confederates built some three thousand cannons, many of which were defective, in comparison to the Union's seven thousand working ones. The Confederacy also managed to provide guns to its troops. In early 1861, the Confederacy began using the gun-making machinery captured at Harpers Ferry to produce arms in Richmond. Still, the Confederacy produced less than 250,000 small arms during the war, while the United States Armory in Springfield, Illinois, produced 800,000. The Union, as a whole, produced over two and a half million small arms during the war. Southerners tried to make up for this arms difference by importing what they could from Europe and by capturing Union rifles. By 1863, they had enough guns for each infantryman to have one.

After the war, one Virginian solider insisted that "they never whipped us, Sir, unless they were four to one. If we had had anything like a fair change, or less disparity of numbers, we should have won our cause and established our independence." Attributing defeat to numerical differences overstates the importance of sheer demographics. Despite its statistical shortcomings, the Confederacy sustained a military force that often equaled and surpassed its Union counterparts from 1861 to 1865. Defeat eventually came to the Confederate army in 1865, but the four years of tightly contested battles attest more to the competitiveness of the war than to the inevitability of a Northern victory.

Unlike the Confederate forces, the Union army was supplied with all the material and equipment it needed to fight a long war of attrition.

Major Battles of the Civil War

The American Civil War began with the expectation on each side that it would quickly emerge victorious. United States President Abraham Lincoln called for 90-day volunteers, while the *New York Times* predicted that this "local commotion" would quickly end "in thirty days." Southerners shared this optimism. "Just throw three or four shells among those blue-bellied Yankees," one North Carolinian declared, "and they'll scatter like sheep." The Civil War did not fulfill early expectations. On July 21, General Irwin McDowell and 30,000 Union soldiers attacked the 20,000 Confederate troops under the command of General P.G.T. Beauregard at Manassas, Virginia. The ensuing battle—which would later be known as the First Battle of Bull Run—was similar to many of the battles that followed in the next four years. The bloody altercation ended in confusion for both sides, blurred the line between victory and defeat, and resulted in massive casualties. Confederate troops declared victory at Bull Run after their Union counterparts retreated, but they were too disorganized to pursue the defeated Federals.

The Civil War lasted for four years after Bull Run, and it took place in at least 16 states and parts of the American territories. These battles occurred in three clusters: the Eastern, Western, and Coastal Theaters. The Eastern Theater involved the most renown battles: Gettysburg, Fredericksburg, Antietam, Bull Run, Chancellorsville, The Wilderness, Spotsylvania, Seven Pines, Cold Harbor, Lynchburg, and Petersburg. Antietam, a battle that occurred in Maryland on September 17, 1862, was the bloodiest day in the Civil War. More Americans died at Antietam than during the other wars the United States fought in the nineteenth century combined. On that day alone, 4,100 soldiers lay dead and over 18,000 were wounded. Approximately three thousand of the wounded would later die from their wounds. The Eastern

The Confederate battle line at Chickamauga. With typical Southern determination General Bragg inflicted over 16,000 casualties on the Union army, though he paid the terrible price of 18,500 of his own irreplaceable soldiers.

Theater also included what many historians believe to be the turning point of the war—Gettysburg. The battle occurred between July 1 and 3, 1863, in Pennsylvania, and it matched Confederate General Robert E. Lee with Union General George G. Meade. The first two days of fighting witnessed Confederate troops failing to dislodge the Union troops from their defensive positions at Cemetery Ridge and Culp's Hill. On July 3, rather than retreat, Lee opted for a frontal assault on the center of the Union lines. After Confederate artillery tried to soften the Union defenses, Lee ordered George E. Pickett to charge 14,000 men up Cemetery Ridge. Pickett's Charge covered nearly a mile of open territory, and it turned into a bloody massacre. Union artillery and rifles killed and wounded nearly all Confederates who made the assault. Many other Southerners surrendered. The Union victory came at the cost of 23,000 dead or wounded, while Lee's men suffered 28,000 casualties.

The Western Theater epitomized the idea that the American Civil War was a total war. The Western Theater included Sherman's March, Shiloh, Fort Henry, Fort Donelson, Kennesaw Mountain, Vicksburg, Olustee, and Fort Pillow. Nathan Bedford Forrest, who would later become the first Grand Wizard of the Ku Klux Klan, used his cavalry to launch surprise attacks against supply lines in the Western Theater, and he obtained a reputation for his innovative cavalry tactics and his unmitigated hostility to Yankee troops and black soldiers. Confederate troops under the command of Forrest murdered black Union soldiers when they surrendered at Fort Pillow, on April 12, 1864. The Union unleashed terrors of their own in the Western Theater. William Tecumseh Sherman's March through Georgia and the Carolinas brought "the hard hand of war" to the South's civilian population. As Sherman and his men crossed the Southern countryside, they burned and destroyed everything that they could. Because the Union targeted many sites on the western waterways—including the Mississippi River and Gulf of Mexico—some campaigns in the Western Theater were joint military-naval operations. For example, Union General Ulysses S. Grant captured Fort Henry on the Tennessee River and then Fort Donelson on the Cumberland River in February 1862 with the help of the Union navy. A similar joint effort also led to the Confederate evacuation of Vicksburg on July 4, 1863.

The third theater of the American Civil War occurred on the water. Although joint military-naval efforts were commonplace, the Union navy had ambitions of its own. Under the leadership of Flag Officer David Farragut, the Union used its navy to establish a blockade and besiege the ports of the Confederacy. The Union occupied New Orleans, South Carolina's Sea Islands, and North Carolina's Roanoke Island by the spring of 1862. The Confederacy mounted a naval defensive, but it was limited by the region's lack of maritime vessels. When the Confederacy seized a navy yard in Norfolk, Virginia, it rebuilt the USS *Merrimack* as an ironclad and renamed it the *Virginia*. The South immediately used its armored vessel to attack the Union blockade. The *Virginia*'s first attack, on March 8, 1862, successfully destroyed two ships and

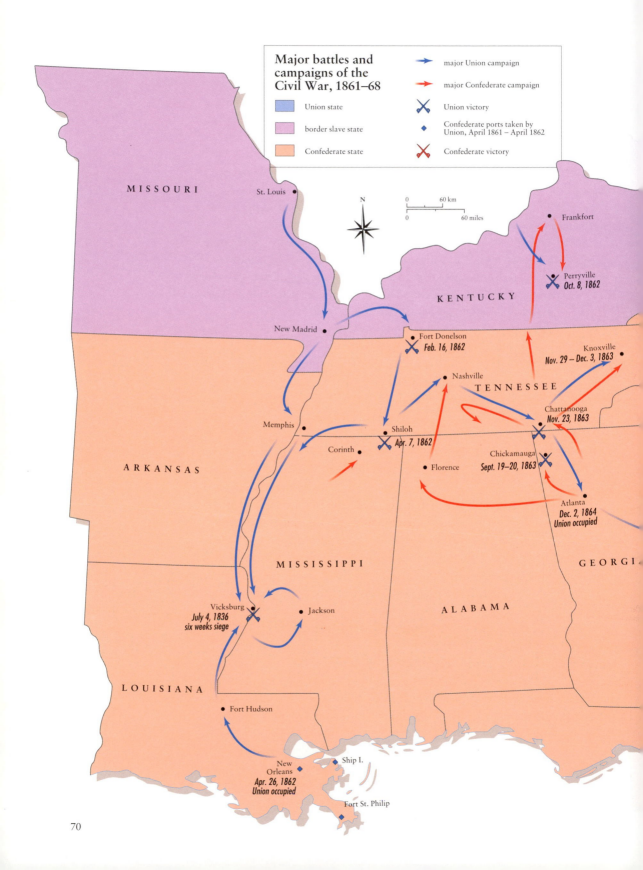

Major battles and campaigns of the Civil War, 1861–68

major Union campaign
major Confederate campaign

Union state
border slave state
Confederate state

Union victory
Confederate ports taken by Union, April 1861 – April 1862
Confederate victory

MISSOURI

St. Louis

KENTUCKY

Frankfort

Perryville
Oct. 8, 1862

New Madrid

Fort Donelson
Feb. 16, 1862

Knoxville
Nov. 29 – Dec. 3, 1863

Nashville

TENNESSEE

Chattanooga
Nov. 23, 1863

Memphis

Shiloh
Apr. 7, 1862

Corinth

Florence

Chickamauga
Sept. 19–20, 1863

ARKANSAS

Atlanta
Dec. 2, 1864
Union occupied

MISSISSIPPI

GEORGIA

ALABAMA

Vicksburg
July 4, 1836
six weeks siege

Jackson

LOUISIANA

Fort Hudson

New
Orleans
Apr. 26, 1862
Union occupied

Ship I.

Fort St. Philip

N

0   60 km
0   60 miles

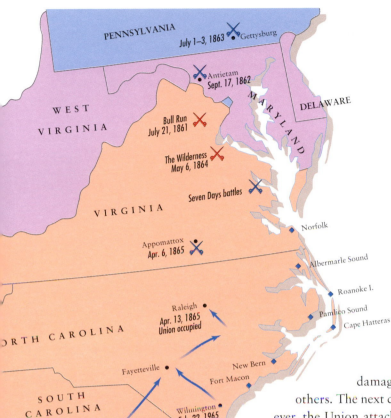

damaged three others. The next day, however, the Union attacked with an ironclad of its own, the *Monitor*. A three-hour engagement between the two ironclads ensued, with neither side able to inflict any damage. The fight between the *Virginia* and the *Monitor* represented the last major challenge to the Union blockade and control of the seas. In the following years, the Union asserted and increased its naval supremacy with the addition of 58 more ironclads to its fleet.

The American Civil War was not the ninety-day affair that Lincoln had foreseen. Nor did the "blue-bellied Yankees . . . scatter like sheep" when the fighting began. The war lasted for four years, from April 1861 to April 1865, and sustained battles occurred in at least 16 of the 36 states. The war took the lives of over 620,000 Americans, amounting then to two percent of the American population. Another 375,000 American soldiers returned home from the war with amputated limbs, physical and emotional scars, and other injuries. Nearly every American family mourned the loss of a relative.

Bull Run

The Confederate decision to move its capital from Montgomery, Alabama, to Richmond, Virginia, brought the two warring capitals within one hundred miles of each other. It also insured that Virginia would become the stage for some of the most important battles of the war. The first major confrontation in Virginia occurred on July 21, 1861, along a small stream called Bull Run, less than thirty miles from Washington, DC. There, under orders from President Abraham Lincoln, General Irvin McDowell and his 30,000 Union soldiers attacked 20,000 Confederates under General P.G.T. Beauregard's command. The rebel troops were stationed at Manassas, a key railroad junction in Virginia, and rumors of an impending attack gave them time to take a defensive position between Manassas and the town of Centreville. Beauregard had hoped to initiate the attack on July 21, but awoke that morning to the sounds of Union artillery.

The battle had been anticipated by both soldiers and civilians for several weeks, and Union troops began to position themselves on July 16. By the time the armies finally engaged each other the morning of Sunday the 21st, they had attracted the curiosity of hundreds of civilian spectators. Carriages from the United States capitol brought congressmen, newspaper correspondents, and other spectators. Some held picnics as they positioned themselves to view the engagement. The genteel men and women of the North prepared to view a historic moment that would presumably reunite the Union and Confederacy. They were not prepared for the horrible reality that would first confront them at Bull Run.

McDowell began to march towards Bull Run hours before dawn. He crossed the Sudley Ford and then deployed his men. The plan was to have this force confront the Confederates and hold them until other troops could outflank and destroy them. Initially, it appeared that this would work. Federal troops hit the outnumbered Confederates' left flank and drove them back. Union troops led by William Tecumseh Sherman joined the fray and hit the flank. The Confederates retreated, regrouped, and began to receive reinforcements at Henry House Hill. There South Carolina General Barnard Bee saw recent Virginia Military Institute instructor Thomas J. Jackson command his well-organized troops, and called upon his men to follow suit. "Look! There is Jackson standing like a stone wall! Rally behind the Virginians!"

Indeed, the Confederates rallied behind the man who became known as "Stonewall" Jackson. For the following two hours, at the peak of the hot and muggy July day, the two armies fought to a bloody standstill. Neither side could move the other from the hill. By four o'clock that afternoon, the Confederates received the last of their reinforcements and once again attacked. The assault began with a legendary rebel yell followed by gunfire, and gradually broke the Union lines. Union troops slowly retreated but panic soon ensued. A retreat turned to a rout. The Union soldiers, tired and scared, stumbled over the picnic baskets and carriages of the startled spectators as they quickly fled the battlefield. When the battled ended, the Union troops regrouped in Washington, DC. The rebel troops, who lacked the horses and wagons to pursue them, remained at the battle site and celebrated their victory.

At day's end, 387 Confederates and 481 Union soldiers were dead, and another 1,582 Confederates and 1,011 Union soldiers were injured. In addition, nearly 1,200 Northern soldiers were captured during the retreat. This was the most costly battle in American history to that point. Unfortunately, this claim would not last long. The battles that followed Bull Run would create casualties that would far exceed the horror experienced that day.

By virtue of Southern victory in the first sustained engagement in the war, many Confederates bragged of their superior martial attributes. They also felt that they had ensured the establishment of independent nationhood. On the following day, the Richmond *Examiner* proclaimed "This blow will shake the Northern Union in every bone; the echo will reverberate round the globe. It secures the independence of the Southern Confederacy. The churches of this city should be open to-day and its inhabitants should render God their thanks for a special providence in their behalf; for yesterday morning the fate of Richmond, with many other fates, trembled in the balance." While Confederates jubilantly proclaimed that this proved that one rebel could whip ten Federals, Lincoln and his leaders concluded that this would not be the ninety-day war they had envisioned. Within the week, Lincoln called for the enlistment of one million Union soldiers.

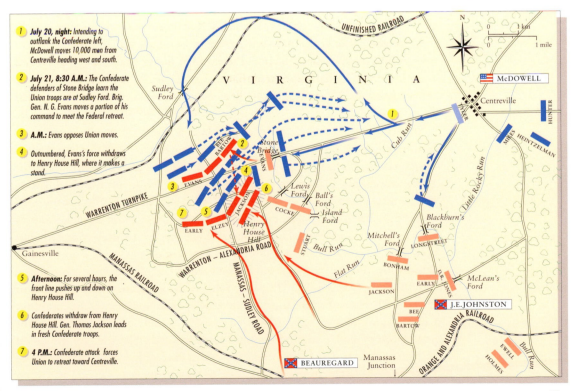

Battle of the Crater

On August 1, 1864, Union General Ulysses Grant lamented that the "disaster on Saturday . . . was the saddest affair I have witnessed in this war." This failed military opportunity—which became known as the Battle of the Crater—began as the brainchild of Lieutenant Colonel Henry Pleasants. Pleasants built a 500-foot mine shaft underneath the Confederate fort that protected Petersburg, Virginia. With the help of coal miners in his regiment, Pleasants placed explosives under the fort that he planned to blow to pieces. He believed a Union victory would then easily follow. Without the support of the army's engineering corps or General George Gordon Meade, who doubted the idea as an engineering impossibility, Pleasants and his men completed the tunnel on July 17. He then filled an underground chamber with 320 kegs or 8,000 pounds of powder. Grant, who only slowly gained a bit of enthusiasm for the tunnel, decided to expand the operation with coordinated assaults by Union artillery and infantrymen. After a victory here, Grant believed he could march straight to Petersburg and destroy the lifeline to the Confederacy's capital, Richmond.

Shortly after midnight on July 30, Union officer Ambrose Burnside readied his divisions to attack the Confederate fort. Burnside hoped to use his black troops to lead the attack, as he was "eager to show the white troops what the colored division could do." Meade objected to the use of the black troops because he feared that defeat would lead to the accusations of intentionally leading black troops to their slaughter. A white division replaced the disappointed black troops at the front lines. At a quarter past three that morning, the Union troops lit the fuse to the underground explosives. When a half hour passed without the expected explosion, Pleasants sent in a couple of men to re-light the fuse. Fifteen minutes later, a tremendous explosion destroyed the fort and its garrison. Pleasants's tunnel performed better than expected. Nearly three hundred Confederates were blown into the air. A huge crater—measuring 60 feet wide, 170 feet long, and 30 feet deep—remained where the fort had recently stood.

Immediately after the initial blast, a Union barrage of 110 heavy cannon and 55 mortars opened fire. After their initial shock, the rebel troops on both sides of the crater retreated from their trenches. Led by Burnside's divisions, the Union troops charged into the heart of the crater. While the awestruck Union troops arrived in the center of the crater, the Confederates regrouped on the crater's mouth. The rebel troops, still somewhat dazed from the blast, slowly began to fire down at the Union soldiers, who were effectively trapped. The crater walls were too steep to climb and the Union troops had no ladders. Burnside responded by sending in Union reinforcements, but they too stormed into the heart of the crater. The crater filled with disorganized and unprepared Union soldiers. By the time the African-American troops entered the crater, the Confederate victory was sealed. The Union withdrawal was met by the Confederate infantry who refused the surrender of the black Union troops. At the end of the day, 3,793 Union soldiers, and 1,182 Confederate soldiers, 287 of whom were killed by the initial blast, lay dead.

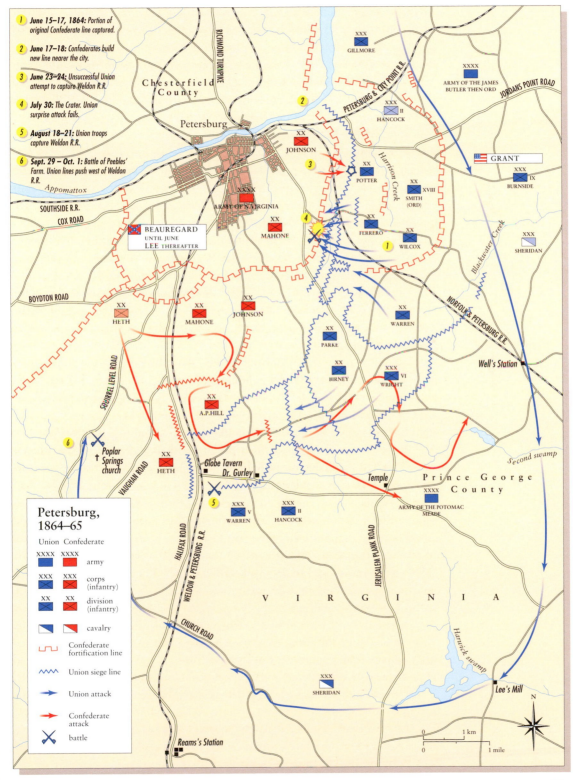

Yankees in the South

In the earliest months of the American Civil War, the Union used the Mississippi River to flood the South with troops. With a near monopoly of naval forces, the Union's armies exploited the natural waterways that pierced the South. One at a time, Union forces captured ports and towns along the Mississippi River and the Atlantic shore. They then used them to establish Union strongholds through the South. The wartime occupation of the South did not occur by water alone, however. Military movements brought Union troops deep into the Southern countryside and into the region's towns and farms. By early 1863, the Union held most of northern Virginia. In addition, federal troops occupied coastal North Carolina, South Carolina, Florida, Louisiana, middle and western Tennessee, and parts of Arkansas, Mississippi, and Alabama. During the course of the war, federal troops occupied over one hundred Southern towns and cities. Even the South's largest cities fell prey to Northern invasion and occupation. New Orleans, Memphis, Nashville, Norfolk, and Alexandria fell near the beginning of the war, and Atlanta, Savannah, Charleston, Richmond, Vicksburg, and Wilmington fell near the end. Countless other areas struggled as Union troops—especially those under General Philip H. Sheridan and General William T. Sherman—placed them under siege, forced their inhabitants to evacuate, and then physically destroyed what was left behind.

The largest Southern city during the war, New Orleans, fell to Union forces in April 1862. Union Naval Commander David G. Farragut led his Gulf Expeditionary Force against the Louisiana port. In addition to the seventeen warships and twenty mortar boats that he commanded, Farragut was aided by General Benjamin F. Butler's 15,000 soldiers. The assault began with a week of mortar shelling, and then, on April 24, Farragut moved his warships up the channel and engaged the forts directly. Confederates sank only one Union ship during the fighting. Overmatched, they soon surrendered to Butler.

Farragut then moved up the Mississippi and captured Natchez, Mississippi, while Butler entered New Orleans and placed it under military rule. Butler quickly earned a reputation among Southerners for his firm, if not corrupt and despotic, occupation. "Beast Butler" confiscated Confederate property—public and private—and he and his brother Andrew made a fortune during his eight-month rule. Butler's implementation of martial law in the city increased his disdain among Southerners. He demanded absolute loyalty to the Union and ordered the execution of one Southerner who tore down an American flag. This did not stop Southern defiance or repress Confederate nationalism. The city's women found countless ways to insult Butler and his occupying forces. They often wore Confederate pins, proclaimed Confederate superiority loudly in the streets, and crossed the street so as not to walk near a Yankee. In one daring move, a Confederate woman emptied her chamber pot on the head of Farragut as he walked under a French Quarter balcony. Such behavior provoked Butler to issue his infamous Woman Order. In it, he declared that all women in New Orleans "shall be regarded and held liable to be treated as a woman of the town plying her avocation." This outraged Southerners and some Northerners, but it did seem to stifle some of the visible and vocal resistance by civilians.

Union occupation did more than incense loyal Southerners. It also impeded the Confederacy's ability to fight the war. When Federal troops occupied the grain- and livestock-producing areas of central Virginia and middle Tennessee, they limited the Confederacy's ability to feed its soldiers and civilians. In addition, the occupation of the port towns prevented Southerners from shipping their cotton to England and France. As Union troops captured Confederate plantations, the United States Congress passed the Captured Property Act in March, 1863, to make it legal to confiscate Confederate-grown cotton. Only Southerners who swore allegiance to the Union could sell their crops. The occupation of Southern towns also led many Southern soldiers to leave their posts and return home where they could protect their property and families from Union depredations.

The occupation of the South had the most profound implications for African-American slaves. The arrival of Federal troops often evoked the cheers of a jubilant slave population who expected to receive their freedom from Union soldiers. As Federal troops marched deeper into the Southern country-side, African-American slaves took the war and their lives into their own hands. They launched small rebellions against their masters, stole weapons and supplies from their plantations and nearby Confederate forces, reported to the Union about Southern troop movements, and even staged labor strikes. Some fugitive slaves engaged in guerrilla warfare against their former masters, but many more simply found freedom behind Union lines. Tens of thousands of slaves used the occupation of their towns and the general wartime disruption to obtain freedom before they were legally emancipated.

The occupied South

- territory controlled by Union, 1861
- Confederate port taken by Union, April 1861 – April 1862
- gained by Union, 1861–62
- gained by Union, 1863
- gained by Union, 1864–65
- territory controlled by Confederacy, 1865

"The Hard Hand of War"

Atlanta after it was burnt down by Sherman's advancing army.

In May 1864, Union General Sherman began a series of maneuvers to force Joseph Johnston's Confederate Army of the Tennessee to retreat toward Atlanta. Sherman's forces, at the start of the Atlanta Campaign, consisted of over 100,000 men in three separate armies: George Thomas's Army of the Cumberland with 61,000 men, James B. McPherson's Army of the Tennessee with 25,000 men, and James M. Schofield's Army of the Ohio with 15,000 men. These armies marched from just south of Chattanooga, Tennessee, and slowly pushed Johnston and his 50,000 troops toward Atlanta. The Union and Confederate armies rarely engaged in direct combat during the ensuing maneuvers, with Sherman opting to orchestrate flanking movements to keep Johnston on the defensive and

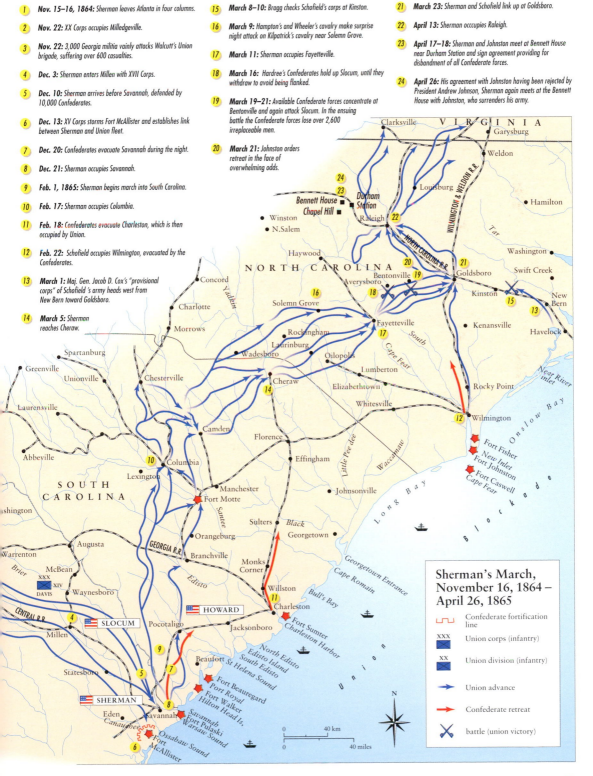

1 *Nov. 15–16, 1864: Sherman leaves Atlanta in four columns.*

2 *Nov. 22: XX Corps occupies Milledgeville.*

3 *Nov. 22: 3,000 Georgia militia vainly attacks Walcutt's Union brigade, suffering over 600 casualties.*

4 *Dec. 3: Sherman enters Millen with XVII Corps.*

5 *Dec. 10: Sherman arrives before Savannah, defended by 10,000 Confederates.*

6 *Dec. 13: XV Corps storms Fort McAllister and establishes link between Sherman and Union fleet.*

7 *Dec. 20: Confederates evacuate Savannah during the night.*

8 *Dec. 21: Sherman occupies Savannah.*

9 *Feb. 1, 1865: Sherman begins march into South Carolina.*

10 *Feb. 17: Sherman occupies Columbia.*

11 *Feb. 18: Confederates evacuate Charleston, which is then occupied by Union.*

12 *Feb. 22: Schofield occupies Wilmington, evacuated by the Confederates.*

13 *March 1: Maj. Gen. Jacob D. Cox's "provisional corps" of Schofield's army heads west from New Bern toward Goldsboro.*

14 *March 5: Sherman reaches Cheraw.*

15 *March 8–10: Bragg checks Schofield's corps at Kinston.*

16 *March 9: Hampton's and Wheeler's cavalry make surprise night attack on Kilpatrick's cavalry near Solemn Grove.*

17 *March 11: Sherman occupies Fayetteville.*

18 *March 16: Hardee's Confederates hold up Slocum, until they withdraw to avoid being flanked.*

19 *March 19–21: Available Confederate forces concentrate at Bentonville and again attack Slocum. In the ensuing battle the Confederate forces lose over 2,600 irreplaceable men.*

20 *March 21: Johnston orders retreat in the face of overwhelming odds.*

21 *March 23: Sherman and Schofield link up at Goldsboro.*

22 *April 13: Sherman occcupies Raleigh.*

23 *April 17–18: Sherman and Johnston meet at Bennett House near Durham Station and sign agreement providing for disbandment of all Confederate forces.*

24 *April 26: His agreement with Johnston having been rejected by President Andrew Johnson, Sherman again meets at the Bennett House with Johnston, who surrenders his army.*

Sherman's March, November 16, 1864 – April 26, 1865

Confederate fortification line

XXX — Union corps (infantry)

XX — Union division (infantry)

→ Union advance

→ Confederate retreat

✕ battle (union victory)

Confederates choosing to retreat rather than risk casualties. On July 17, Johnston was blamed by General Robert E. Lee for Sherman's repeated advances and was relieved of his command. John B. Hood replaced him with the Confederate government's expectation that he would take the offensive. The series of Confederate retreats quickly ended, with Hood leading three consecutive assaults on Sherman's forces. Each assault ended with heavy casualties and as strategic disasters for the Confederates. In the end, Sherman laid siege to Atlanta.

The siege of Atlanta lasted until August, with Union artillery constantly bombarding the city while Hood and Sherman tried to outmaneuver each other. On August 25, Sherman led Hood to believe that he had grown weary of the fight and had retreated. Hours after Hood telegraphed Richmond with news of Sherman's retreat, Union troops attacked the railroads on the southside of Atlanta. Union troops melted the tracks and wrapped them around surrounding trees—what troops referred to as "Sherman neckties." Hood's response to the surprise attack came too late; Sherman had already cut off Atlanta. On September 1, the day after the Confederates attacked Sherman and tried to recapture the railroad, Hood decided to evacuate Atlanta. Before they left the city, the Confederate troops destroyed anything of military value that they could not otherwise carry. A battered Atlanta fell into Sherman's hands. Sherman would occupy Atlanta until November 15, and he left the town in flames. Nearly one third of Atlanta was destroyed by the fire, including most of the business district.

The destruction of the Southern home front did not end with the taking and burning of Atlanta. Convinced that "we are not only fighting hostile armies, but a hostile people," Sherman actively sought to destroy the will of the Southern civilians. To this end, he sought and received permission from President Lincoln to begin a march from Atlanta to Savannah. Sherman left Atlanta on November 15 with 62,000 Union soldiers. As they crossed the countryside, soldiers burned plantations, stole food and livestock, and generally terrorized civilians. Sherman and his men marched ten miles a day, a pace that gave them time to destroy the areas they passed through. Along their 300-mile-long and 60-mile-wide path, Sherman and his troops wreaked a destruction so complete that "a crow flying over it would have to carry his own rations." Confederates abandoned Savannah on December 21, and the following day Sherman placed the city under Union rule. Sherman graciously sent word to President Lincoln of his victory. "I beg to present to you, as a Christmas gift, the city of Savannah, with one hundred and fifty heavy guns, and plenty of ammunition, also about twenty-five thousand bales of cotton."

In February, Sherman and his men left Savannah and began a 50-day, and 425-mile march through South Carolina. Rains and swamps slowed down the Union forces, but they did not deter the campaign. The path of destruction in the Palmetto State was even more devastating than that in Georgia. South Carolina, Sherman reasoned, as the initiator of secession and Civil War, deserved to "feel the hard hand of war." One of Sherman's infantrymen agreed. "Here is where treason began," he wrote. "By God, here is where it shall end!" Consequently, Sherman destroyed the railroads that led to Augusta and Charleston, and on February 18, Charleston surrendered. Black Union soldiers entered the city first, singing "John Brown's Body" as they extinguished the fires that the Confederates had lit before they evacuated. Columbia, the city Sherman targeted after Charleston fell, was not as lucky. Nearly half of the city was in ashes the morning after Sherman's men arrived. The cause of the fires is still debated today, as some fires were accidentally set by Confederates when they burned their cotton. The Union's inability or refusal to extinguish the fires resulted in the city's destruction. As Sherman continued on to North Carolina, Confederate forces under General Johnston tried to stop him. These efforts were of no avail. Outnumbered, on March 19, Johnston attacked Sherman's left wing. After a day-long standstill, the Confederate troops retreated northward. The march through Georgia and the Carolinas was over.

Confederate captives await transfer to a Federal prison camp.

The South Surrenders

The destruction of Confederate resources by Sherman's march left the Southern home front in shambles. The campaign of razing and plundering pursued by Union troops destroyed the South's ability to provide its soldiers with clothing, food, and other supplies. Other Confederate defeats added to a growing crisis of confidence. When springtime approached in 1865, the Union had reclaimed or destroyed most of the territory once controlled by the Confederacy. In addition, desertion from the Confederate ranks swelled to epidemic proportions, and other Southerners rejected urgent calls for their enlistment.

Amidst this crisis of morale and manpower, Confederate leaders did not abandon the struggle for Southern independence. Their fight, however, grew

Appomattox, April 2–6 1865

→ Union advance

→ Confederate advance

✕ battle

Union	Confederate	
XXX	XXX	corps (infantry)
XX	XX	division (infantry)
▰	▰	cavalry

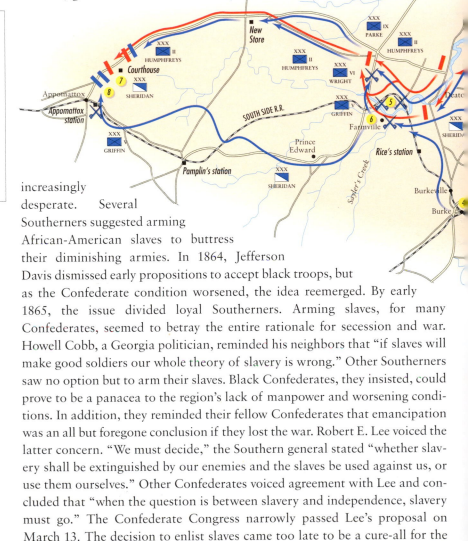

increasingly desperate. Several Southerners suggested arming African-American slaves to buttress their diminishing armies. In 1864, Jefferson Davis dismissed early propositions to accept black troops, but as the Confederate condition worsened, the idea reemerged. By early 1865, the issue divided loyal Southerners. Arming slaves, for many Confederates, seemed to betray the entire rationale for secession and war. Howell Cobb, a Georgia politician, reminded his neighbors that "if slaves will make good soldiers our whole theory of slavery is wrong." Other Southerners saw no option but to arm their slaves. Black Confederates, they insisted, could prove to be a panacea to the region's lack of manpower and worsening conditions. In addition, they reminded their fellow Confederates that emancipation was an all but foregone conclusion if they lost the war. Robert E. Lee voiced the latter concern. "We must decide," the Southern general stated "whether slavery shall be extinguished by our enemies and the slaves be used against us, or use them ourselves." Other Confederates voiced agreement with Lee and concluded that "when the question is between slavery and independence, slavery must go." The Confederate Congress narrowly passed Lee's proposal on March 13. The decision to enlist slaves came too late to be a cure-all for the ailing South. The war ended less than a month later.

While Confederates considered including African-American soldiers in their military, Richmond fell into Union hands. The loss of the Confederate capital confirmed fears that Southern independence could not be achieved. Lee tried to save his army of 35,000 by marching them away from Richmond and the Union forces. He hoped to join General Joseph E. Johnston and regroup in the west.

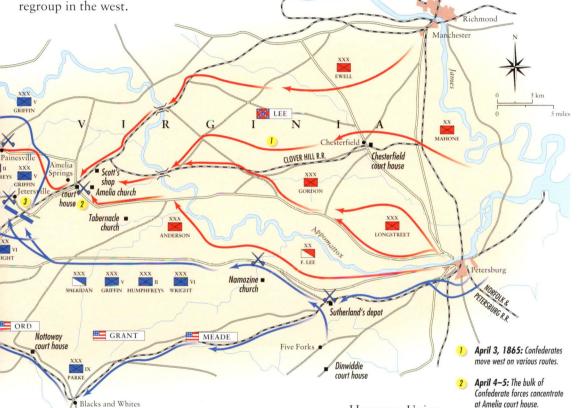

However, Union troops pursued Lee, and, on April 6 over seven thousand Confederates were forced to surrender at Sayler's Creek. For nearly two days, Union troops captured hundreds of exhausted Confederate stragglers who could not keep up with Lee's army. On April 8, Union General Philip Sheridan captured two trainloads of rations that awaited the Confederates at Appomattox Station, Virginia. Lee reluctantly concluded that he had no option but to surrender. "There is nothing left for me to do but to go and see General [Ulysses S.] Grant," Lee somberly stated. "I would rather die a thousand deaths." On April 9, Lee surrendered to Grant at Appomattox Courthouse. Grant offered his Confederate foe generous conditions of surrender. He allowed Lee's men to return their homes without punishment and allowed them to take their horses so that they could "put in a crop." Lee accepted the terms and his soldiers dispersed.

1. **April 3, 1865:** Confederates move west on various routes.

2. **April 4–5:** The bulk of Confederate forces concentrate at Amelia court house.

3. **April 5:** Union forces arrive near Jetersville and block Confederate movement south along the railroad.

4. **April 5, late:** Ord's Army of the James arrives at Burke.

5. **April 6:** Battle of Sayler's Creek. Confederate rear guard is cut off and 6,000 men captured.

6. **April 7:** Battle of Farmville. Confederates repulse Union attack and cross Appomattox.

7. **April 8, p.m.:** Confederates concentrate at Appomattox Courthouse.

8. **April 9:** Lee surrenders to Grant.

From Slavery to Freedom

While the American Civil War was still being fought, former slave turned abolitionist orator Frederick Douglass worried that the outcome of the Civil War might not necessarily be of concern to the slaves themselves. Too many Northerners, he reasoned, were as much against the institution of slavery as its abolition and too often "the drift of northern sentiment was towards compromise." As a result, he worried that African-American slaves might remain in bondage even if the war ended with a Union victory. Yet Douglass had no choice but to support the war. As the war progressed, the aims of the United States slowly expanded to include abolition. After Robert E. Lee finally surrendered to Ulysses S. Grant at Appomattox, Frederick Douglass could write "From the first, I, for one, saw in this war the end of slavery, and truth requires me to say that my interest in the success of the North was largely due to this belief. True it is that this faith was many times shaken by passing events, but never destroyed." Douglass's earlier fears were not realized and now forgotten. A war initially designed to save the Union had became a war that also freed the slaves.

Douglass had real reasons for his initial lamentations. The United States' and Abraham Lincoln's ultimate decision to make the Civil War about slavery evolved slowly and unevenly. Although Lincoln declared before his 1860 election that he believed slavery was "an unqualified evil to the negro, the white man, and the State," he also concluded that the Constitution did not give the President the power to act on the institution. In his inaugural address, partially as an attempt to soothe the fears of the border states, Lincoln proclaimed that he had "no purpose, directly, or indirectly, to interfere with slavery in the States where it exists." Over the next two years, however, Lincoln's "purpose" changed in response to the pressures of war and abolitionists in his Republican Party.

At the outset of the Civil War, Lincoln refrained from maneuvers that even hinted at emancipation. He recognized that such acts would strengthen the resolve of Confederates and possibly convince border states, especially Maryland, to abandon the Union. Perhaps even more importantly, talk of emancipation scared many Northern whites whose disdain for the institution did not preclude an equal disdain for African-Americans. Lincoln, throughout the early part of the war, proclaimed the need to preserve the Union rather than to free the slaves. He ordered his generals to return runaway slaves to their Southern masters, and insisted that the preservation of the Union superseded all other concerns.

David C. Barrow's Syll's Fork plantation, Oglethorpe County, Georgia

woodland

1860

Little River

Wright's Branch

gin house
master's house
slave quarters

Branch Creek

Syll's Fork

As the war progressed, Lincoln's attitude towards slavery changed. From a practical standpoint, the President recognized that African-American slaves increased the Confederacy's ability to fight. They helped cultivate food and cotton, performed manual labor for the rebel army, and worked in several of the South's munitions factories. In the first year of the war, General Benjamin Butler recognized the slave's asset to the Confederacy and used it to further his abolitionist aims. When three slaves escaped from Confederate lines where they had been building rebel fortifications, Butler "seized" them and called them "contraband of war." As property, Butler concluded, these slaves could be seized like any other spoils of war. In addition, they could not be tactically returned to their masters because they would further the ability of the South to win. Butler proclaimed, somewhat ironically, that he could free the slaves if they were treated as property instead of as humans. Lincoln condemned Butler's decision, but over the next year "contrabands" flooded Union camps. The occasional practice by some Union commanders of returning these escapees to their masters ended when Congress finally forbade the return of runaway slaves in March, 1862.

During the ensuing months, Republican supporters pressured Lincoln to turn the war against the slaveholding South into a war against slavery. In July, Congress passed a confiscation act, which freed the slaves of those persons engaged in rebellion. It also passed a law that allowed freed slaves to work and fight for the Union army. Then in September, 1862, Lincoln announced that he planned to issue an emancipation proclamation on January 1, 1863 if the rebellion had not yet ended. Although this order would not affect slaves living within the Union's border states, every slave within the Confederate states had his or her future linked to the outcome of the Civil War. As Lincoln wrote, emancipation was "a military necessity. . . . We must free the slaves or be ourselves subdued." Douglass's earlier fears were eased. The Civil War had evolved into what the radical abolitionists wanted in the first place—an assault on the Southern slaveocracy.

By the war's end, the Senate and its Republican majority approved abolishing slavery within the United States with the passing of the Thirteenth Amendment. When this amendment was sent to the newly reunited states for ratification, at least four former Confederate states needed to support it for the necessary two-thirds majority. To insure ratification, President Andrew Johnson made its acceptance a precondition for Confederate states to restore their position in the Union. Three quarters of the states finally ratified the thirteenth amendment by December 18, 1865.

PART IV: THE NEW SOUTH

The American Civil War destroyed simultaneously the Confederacy and its "cornerstone" of African slavery. Former slave and abolitionist Frederick Douglass understood both the importance and the limits of such a revolutionary moment. "The work" he stated "does not end with the abolition of slavery, but only begins." As Douglass astutely observed, the futures of African-American freedmen and of the American South had hardly been determined by the Civil War. These issues would be addressed during the period of Reconstruction that immediately followed the war and then further resolved during the decades called the New South. The first period lasted until 1877, and it was largely controlled by the federal government, black Southerners, and Northerners. During Reconstruction, it appeared that the postwar South might undergo a complete reorganization. The second period represented a return to home rule of the South. The gains made by many African-Americans in the immediate aftermath of the war were reversed by white Southerners who built the region in the images of their choosing. As W.E.B. Du Bois lamented: "the slave went free; stood a brief moment in the sun; then moved back again toward slavery."

For Douglass, Du Bois, and others, the most pressing issue after the American Civil War concerned the nearly four million former slaves who had recently obtained their freedom. Emancipation and citizenship—granted by the Thirteenth, Fourteenth, and Fifteenth Amendments—did not necessarily signify political, economic, or social equality for black Southerners. During the initial years of Reconstruction, President Johnson seemed unconcerned for the plight of the freedmen. Republican congressmen eventually wrested control from the executive branch and began to address some of the needs of Southern blacks. New policies protected the liberties of African-Americans and freed up federal funds to restructure the region. Southern blacks enjoyed access to the ballot box, and hundreds of black public officials were elected in the 1870s. Policies also protected the ability of Southern blacks to marry, file court cases, serve on juries, relocate, and obtain educations. African-American families who had been separated during slavery reunited, and thousands of former slaves formally changed their names to reflect their new freedom. In addition, Southern blacks formed independent churches, schools, fraternal organizations, equal rights leagues, and burial societies.

The end of Reconstruction in 1877 was followed by a complete repudiation of these liberties. Southern blacks remained free in the New South era, but the meaning of this freedom was severely curtailed. Poll taxes, grandfather clauses, literacy tests, understanding clauses, and physical intimidation resulted in the complete disfranchisement of Southern blacks. Vagrancy laws restricted the mobility of blacks, and Jim Crow segregation laws brought racial inequality to nearly every aspect of Southern life. Interaction between the races was governed by an extensive code that expected blacks to be submissive, docile, and dependent. Lynchings and other forms of extralegal violence were used by Southern whites to enforce the region's new racial etiquette. Some blacks tried to escape the New South conditions by migrating north during World War I, but most African-Americans simply endured the postwar realities.

The limited meaning of freedom for emancipated African-Americans resulted partly from the region's inequitable division of land. Black Southerners—with few exceptions—did not benefit from policies of land redistribution during Reconstruction or the New South. Former slaves received their freedom, but they primarily remained poor and landless. As a result, Southern blacks had few alternatives for employment other than working for the region's landed masters. Cultivation of cotton remained the region's central source of employment, and white landowners controlled this economic arena. The labor systems that emerged in the Reconstruction South and the New South—primarily sharecropping and tenant farming—brought black laborers and white landowners back together. In many ways, these labor systems resembled the Old South's system of slavery. White landowners limited the ability of their black fieldhands to negotiate better work conditions, and they used a system of debts to prevent their laborers from physically moving. African-Americans attempted to shape this new labor system to their own desires by controlling their family's labor and by avoiding gang labor. Nevertheless, the inability of Southern blacks to purchase their own land severely curtailed their ability to make the New South look remarkably different from the Old.

The restructuring of the American South was not entirely connected to the questions of labor and race relations. In the aftermath of the American Civil War, Southerners and Northerners alike tried to restructure the Southern economy. The postwar modernization of the Southern economy occurred with mixed success. New towns and cities appeared in the aftermath of the American Civil War, but the South remained entrenched in its rural background. New industries also appeared in the New South—especially lumber, cigarettes, textiles, iron, and turpentine. Yet a complete overhaul of the region's economy did not occur. The region's industrial base remained connected to its rural strengths, and the region's economy remained connected to cotton.

Amid the rhetorical clamors for change and the creation of a New South, white Southerners recreated a new world that in many ways resembled the old. The institution of slavery was abolished, but sharecropping replicated many of its most abusive aspects. Blacks' geographic mobility was curtailed by debts and vagrancy laws. Slave codes were eliminated in the aftermath of the war, but Black Codes, Jim Crow legislation, and disfranchisement quickly took their place. African-Americans, who were landless slaves prior to the war, remained landless laborers in its aftermath. Southern boosters sought to modernize the South, but industrial growth remained confined to the region's agricultural strengths. Urbanization also altered the Southern countryside, but the rest of the nation was changing at an even greater pace. Even planter dominance survived the American Civil War. Many of the wholesale changes that appeared during Reconstruction would not return until the Civil Rights Movement in the 1960s.

Reconstruction

Republican sympatizer Thomas Nast expresses his disapproval of the Reconstruction policy in this Shakespearian style cartoon, featuring President Johnson as Iago and a Union veteran as Othello.

When Lincoln died in April, 1865, the nation lost the President who had guided the nation through the Civil War and promised to create postwar unity with "malice toward none; with charity for all." Thrust into Lincoln's place, President Andrew Johnson immediately battled the antagonistic Republican-controlled Senate to determine the future of the United States. Although the Emancipation Proclamation ended the nation's use of chattel slavery, the future condition of African-Americans had not yet been determined. Lincoln had publicly endorsed limited suffrage for Southern blacks just days before his death, but this did not sit easy with many Americans. The status of former Confederate states, soldiers, politicians, and supporters had not been determined either. In addition, the uncertainty of the Southern economy and the destruction of the Southern countryside demanded governmental attention.

In May 1865, Johnson began an era of Presidential Reconstruction that lasted for two years. He offered immediate pardons to all white Southerners, except for those who held leadership positions in the Confederacy or were wealthy planters. These individuals had to ask Johnson for individual pardons. Johnson granted over 14,000 of these special pardons. As a condition of readmittance to the Union, Southern governments needed to abolish slavery, repudiate secession, and invalidate their Confederate debts. Except for these requirements, Johnson offered little guidance for the reshaping of Southern society. He offered no solution for landless African-American freedmen, and rejected calls to provide former slaves "forty acres and a mule." The resumption of political power by ex-Confederates outraged many Northerners, especially Republican congressmen and former abolitionists. The emerging Black Codes—laws that required African-Americans to sign labor contracts to white landowners and limited other freedoms of former slaves—further undermined Republican support for Johnson.

In late 1865, Radical Republicans effectively dissolved the state governments formed under Johnson's plan and ordered the Southern states to establish governments based on legal equality and manhood suffrage. The radicals did not win this battle, and instead moderate Republicans modified Johnson's plan to their liking. In early 1866, they pushed for the extension of the Freedmen's Bureau and a Civil Rights bill that declared that all persons born in the United States were citizens and entitled to all of the rights inherent to such status. By June, both houses of Congress had approved the Fourteenth Amendment—which made former slaves citizens. Congress overrode Johnson's vetoes of the Freedmen's Bureau, that provided food, shelter, education, and medical assistance to former slaves.

By 1867, the direction of Reconstruction had changed again. Congress, irritated by Johnson's policies, passed the Reconstruction Acts of 1867. With these acts came a new era, one of Radical Reconstruction. Congress split the South into five military districts and explicitly determined how Southern governments would be established. A Union general who had the power to "suppress insurrection, disorder, and violence" controlled each district. Within each district, federal troops protected the legal rights of African-Americans and ensured the registration of black voters. In February, 1869, Congress prohibited the practice of voting laws which inhibited participation based on race.

In this manner, the Union eventually readmitted all Confederate states to the Union by 1870. African-Americans, who formed the overwhelming majority of the electorate, successfully supported many black officials. Sixteen African-Americans served in Congress, over six hundred worked as state legislators, and others filled local offices throughout the South. African-Americans entered the political ranks in ways that had been unthinkable. Although hampered by the economic devastation in the region, the Reconstruction governments called for the economic uplifting of former slaves, ensured that juries were composed of the accused's peers, created the South's first state-funded public schools, increased the bargaining power of agricultural laborers, and outlawed racial discrimination in public transportation and accommodations.

Despite these apparent successes, Radical Reconstruction did not even please all of the radicals. The federal government never confiscated the plantations of the South's wealthiest supporters, nor did it redistribute lands among the freed slaves. This left freedmen in an unenviable and disadvantaged position and the former slaveowners in a familiar one. "Give us our own land and we take care of ourselves, but without land" one former slave knew that "the old masters can hire us or starve us, as they please." Even as these economic realities forced poor blacks back onto the region's plantations as hired field and house laborers, freedmen tried to instill their newfound freedom with as much meaning as possible. In the pursuit of economic independence and cultural autonomy, freedmen reunited families, legalized marriages, abandoned slave quarters for independent households, and created separate African-American churches. The gains made by many African-Americans during Reconstruction would not last.

This reversion began even before Reconstruction officially came to an end. Violent reprisals by the recently formed Ku Klux Klan terrified many Southern towns and tried to impose a new order upon the region. Radical Reconstruction lost more momentum as moderate Republicans shied away from the racial egalitarianism and the ever-expanding power of the federal government. When Democrats won control of the House of Representatives in 1874, Southern voters returned power to the hands of white Democrats. When the returns for 1876 election between Republican Rutherford B. Hayes and Democrat Samuel J. Tilden left the outcome in dispute, a secret compromise settled both the election and the future of Reconstruction. In return for a Republican presidential victory, the federally controlled Reconstruction era came to an end, and Democrats returned as the party of the South.

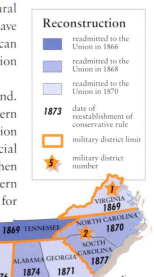

Reconstruction

- readmitted to the Union in 1866
- readmitted to the Union in 1868
- readmitted to the Union in 1870
- *1873* date of reestablishment of conservative rule
- military district limit
- ⑤ military district number

Industrializing Dixie

A Southern sugar refinery. Along with tobacco, manufactured into cigaretttes, sugar, and cotton were the original mainstays of Southern industry.

The withdrawal of Federal troops in 1877 left the South in a precarious position between the old and the new. With the cornerstone of the Confederacy and the Old South now forever abolished, some Southerners envisioned industry as leading to the rise of a powerful and modern New South. Southerners never formulated a single image of what the New South would be, but industrial development became one of its foundations. Henry W. Grady, editor of the Atlanta *Constitution* and one of the most vocal supporters of the "New South Creed," proclaimed in 1886 that "the old South rested everything on slavery and agriculture, unconscious that these could neither give nor maintain healthy growth. The new South presents a perfect democracy, the oligarchs leading in the popular movement—a social system compact and closely knitted, less splendid on the surface, but stronger at the core—a hundred farms for every plantation, fifty homes for every palace—and a diversified industry that meets the complex need of this complex age." This New South Creed turned the region completely upside down, Grady declared. The agrarian ways of the Old South would have to be modified to fit the postwar order. Southerners must retain regional pride but fully enter the industrial age; they must preserve their agricultural past but turn it into an industrial advantage.

Grady, like other promoters of Southern industry, exaggerated the postwar changes within the South. Industry came to the South in ways that it had never done before, but the region remained dependent on northeastern finances and deeply rooted in its agricultural past. Too many disadvantages—Northern entrenchment in most industries, Southern inexperience in manufacturing, high interest rates in the region, cautious state governments, and unfavorable federal banking policies—prevented a full-fledged emergence of Southern industry. Still, Southerners managed to turn their agricultural advantages into some industrial successes. For example, tobacco, especially with James Buchanan Duke's introduction of the Bonsack cigarette rolling machine in 1884, brought new opportunities to the region. Following the example of the Robber Barons in the North, Duke used rebates, price manipulation, and a centralized corporate structure to capture the cigarette market. "If John D. Rockefeller can do what he is doing for oil," Duke explained "why should I not do it in tobacco." In 1890, Duke monopolized the industry by uniting his four biggest competitors under the American Tobacco Company. By 1900, he produced nearly all of the nation's cigarettes, and his American Tobacco Company amounted to a five-hundred-million-dollar trust.

The region's success in cigarette manufacturing was equaled by other agriculturally based industries. Furniture makers capitalized on the region's ample lumber supply. North Carolina, for example, which had six factories in 1890, boasted forty-four a decade later. The region also began to produce the majority of some of the nation's building supplies: bricks, doors, windows, precut lumber, and shingles. In addition, the South also experienced great innovations in the field of mining. At the end of the

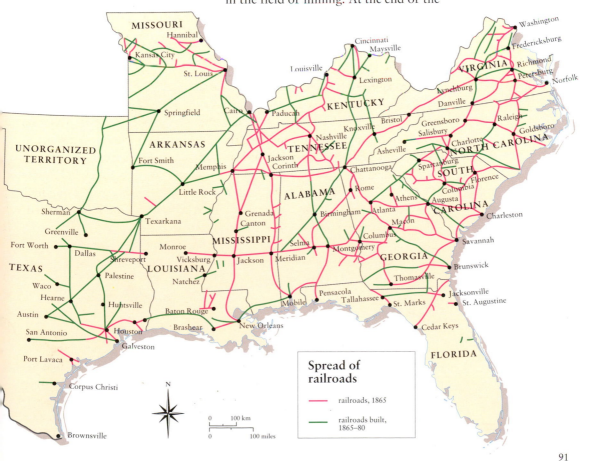

Spread of railroads

—— railroads, 1865

—— railroads built, 1865–80

nineteenth century, many Southerners believed that phosphates, coal, and iron would soon transform the region and bring it up to modern Northern standards. Birmingham emerged as the region's pig iron capital, but its profitability quickly declined with the emergence of steel. Although mining failed to live up to the grandest expectations, the existence of natural minerals did change parts of the region.

The greatest modernizing achievements were made in Southern textile mills. In the decades after Reconstruction, the South captured some of the textile market which had been dominated by New England for decades. In 1870, the South had only eight percent of the nation's textile workers, but in 1900 it boasted nearly one third of these workers, and its mills accounted for sixty percent of the cloth exported from the United States. As the region's mills increasingly benefited from

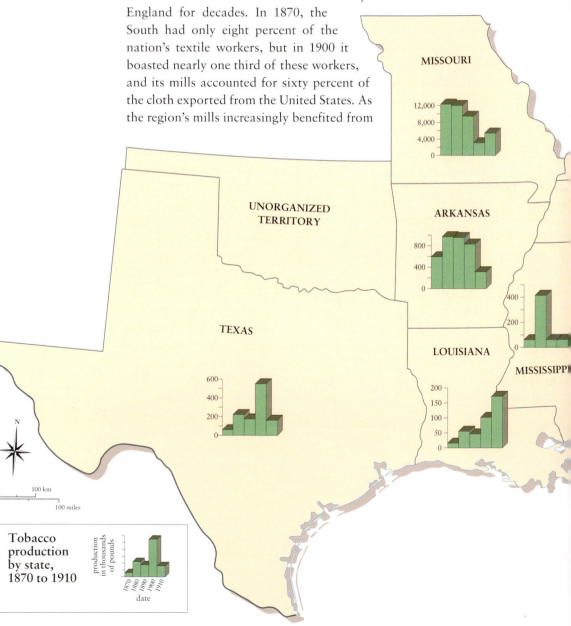

Tobacco production by state, 1870 to 1910

production in thousands of pounds

date

steam power, the number of textile workers and mills skyrocketed. Between 1870 and 1900, the number of Southerners working in textiles increased nine-fold, from 10,000 to 90,000. During the same time, the number of mills approximately doubled. From the eve of secession, South Carolina quadrupled, Georgia tripled and North Carolina doubled their previous record textile out-puts.

Railroads which had been largely destroyed or disabled during the Civil War were rebuilt and expanded to facilitate the increase in industry. By 1900, nearly every Southern town had access to the rails.

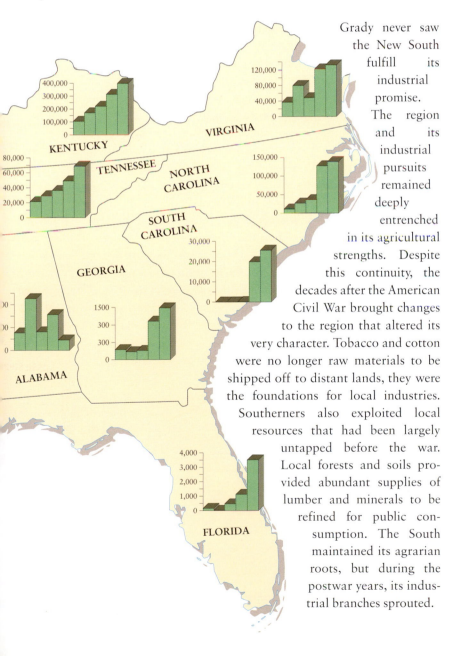

Grady never saw the New South fulfill its industrial promise. The region and its industrial pursuits remained deeply entrenched in its agricultural strengths. Despite this continuity, the decades after the American Civil War brought changes to the region that altered its very character. Tobacco and cotton were no longer raw materials to be shipped off to distant lands, they were the foundations for local industries. Southerners also exploited local resources that had been largely untapped before the war. Local forests and soils provided abundant supplies of lumber and minerals to be refined for public consumption. The South maintained its agrarian roots, but during the postwar years, its industrial branches sprouted.

The Urbanization of the Agrarian South

Sherman's 1864 burning of Atlanta razed an emerging town of 9,500 residents. A new city arose literally from the ashes. Within three years, its mayor, James E. Williams, rejoiced that "a little over one year [had] passed" since the rebuilding of the business district began, "and how changed the scene. The city has been rebuilt and our thronged streets and active mechanics and businessmen indicate that Atlanta fresh from her smoldering ruins of the past . . . is again on the way to prosperity." Atlanta was quickly becoming a major depot for four railroad companies. To Williams's chagrin, however, the prosperity born of urbanization would not immediately arrive in Atlanta or other Southern cities. The Civil War merely turned a rural region with slaves into a rural region without slaves. The rhetoric of urban boosters could not match the reality of a persistent agrarian region. In 1900, less than one in six Southerners lived in towns, and most Southerners continued to enjoy an agrarian style of life.

Despite the persistence of ruralism, the Southern landscape did not remain the same. In the decades after Reconstruction, New South cities grew where small towns or farms had once existed. The spread of industry and railroads throughout the southeast sponsored this urban growth. Located primarily in the region's interior and west, these new cities became commercial centers and places to find financial, governmental, and legal services. Southern cities became progressive locales, places for entrepreneurs and professionals to congregate. Like Atlanta, which eventually became the region's leading metropolis, other interior areas flourished as a result of the railroad. Louisville, Nashville, Montgomery, Charlotte, Memphis, Richmond, Dallas, San Antonio, Houston, Birmingham, and Columbia all arose not out of antebellum ashes but out of iron and coal. Each Southern city had its own causes of growth. For example, the manufacturing and marketing of steel transformed Birmingham, Alabama, from a cornfield in 1871 to a town of 3,086 in 1880 and a bustling city of 132,685 in 1910.

New South cities were often the creations of urban boosters. These financiers built and attracted railroad lines to foster economic development and urban growth in the region. Often, the same local boosters opened prominent hotels in Southern cities to attract business. Investors financed the urban infrastructure. Cities suffered from their uneven development and lack of municipal planning. In 1892, Atlanta boasted the Equitable Building, the region's first skyscraper, but the city mostly

Urbanization

- town with 5,000 to 25,000 inhabitants
- town with over 25,000 inhabitants

1860

0   200 km

0   200 miles

contained unpaved roads, inadequate sewer systems, a private police force, unorganized fire control, and few public parks or schools. In addition, many urbanites kept chickens, horses, cows, hogs, and other animals. Few Southern cities had access to clean water, instead relying on polluted private wells and cisterns. In many cities, these conditions led to the virulent spread of diseases. In addition to suffering from alarming rates of infant mortality, several cities were plagued by deadly epidemics. In 1878-1879, for example, almost six thousand died in the Memphis yellow fever scourge. The disruption was so great that it forced the city into bankruptcy and convinced hundreds of German residents to migrate to nearby St. Louis.

Although some Southern cities actively tried to attract European immigrants, New South cities predominately grew as a result of urban migration from Southern farms. Immediately after the Civil War, many Southerners, especially freed blacks, moved to the cities in the hopes of finding better opportunities than those in rural areas. Economic depression slowed this migration in the 1870s, but it resumed again in the following decade. By 1890, fifteen percent of all Southern blacks lived in cities, and a decade later fifteen percent of all Southerners were urbanites. Although interior New South cities tended quickly to segregate African-Americans into underpaid occupations and run-down communities, Southern blacks still viewed the city as a place of expanded opportunities. If nothing else, it was an escape from the plantation with its slavery-associated cotton agriculture and sharecropping.

Whites responded to the influx of black residents with the weapons of Jim Crow after the 1880s. However, exclusion from restaurants, train stations, and other public facilities did not deter the African-American migration. Even though skilled African-American artisans frequently found career opportunities limited by racist hiring practices, every Southern city witnessed the rise of a black professional class. Black lawyers, teachers, doctors, and other professionals ran their own hospitals, banks, schools, burial societies, churches, insurance companies, and fraternal organizations such as the Colored Masons and United Daughters of Ham within their own communities.

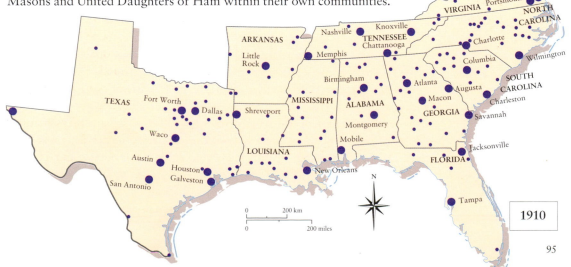

Cotton Culture and Sharecropping

The Emancipation Proclamation and the Thirteenth Amendment destroyed the institution of slavery that had been the cornerstone of the Southern economy for nearly two centuries. However, the region's postwar reconstruction left intact the region's reliance on cotton. Securing the continued survival of King Cotton and the economic supremacy of white landowners required a new labor force. Reestablishing race slavery was impossible, and attracting immigrant workers to the agrarian South was difficult. Without fieldhands to turn their fertile soils into the profitable cash crops, Southern planters faced an economic and cultural crisis. Rather than looking to the North for a solution to their problem, former masters looked to their past. Once again, white landowners found a way to use African-Americans to meet their labor needs.

After Reconstruction, African-Americans faced a crisis of their own. Discussions in Congress and on the plantations for redistributing the region's wealth to give every slave family "forty acres and a mule" never came to fruition. Although some Southerners lost their landholdings during the war, these losses usually resulted in gains for the white creditors who repossessed them. The few Southerners who had their lands confiscated by occupying Union troops during the Civil War had their property returned to them when the war ended. African-Americans, who rarely owned land in the antebellum South, continued to be shut out of the postwar real estate market. Those that obtained land during Reconstruction usually found themselves evicted by Southern officials in the 1880s. Landless and unemployed, recently freed blacks needed to find a means of obtaining the food, clothing, and shelter that their masters once provided. African-Americans had obtained freedom from slavery but did not necessarily secure their independence from the region's white landowners.

Sharecropping emerged out of these reciprocal crises as a form of compromise between landowner and laborer. In return for a share of the crop, usually an equal or one-half split, landowners rented individual portions of their plantations to freedmen and their families. Within this system, African-Americans preserved some of the liberties they gained during Reconstruction. Blacks were free, at least in theory, to find the best labor arrangement that they could. They could negotiate with various landowners, and in essence the system allowed them to choose their boss. Not surprisingly, many sharecroppers rented their land from someone other than their former master. Sharecropping also provided African-Americans the ability to use their family as the basic unit of agricultural labor. African-American families could organize their labor according to the fluctuating demands of the harvest and their personal desires. In addition, Southern blacks avoided gang labor, controlled their work hours, moved into family homes far from the

TEXAS

planter's home, and created social distance between a flourishing black community and former masters.

The system of sharecropping, although shaped by the efforts by African-Americans to create autonomy and independence, heavily favored Southern white landowners. Rental agreements forced sharecroppers to work long hours and endure poor living conditions if they wanted to survive. In addition, the system kept most blacks in a cycle of perpetual poverty. Some landlords charged exorbitant prices for tools, clothing, and food. Planters provided the credit for these supplies and employed interest rates that often reached twenty-five percent. Escaping this economic system proved difficult and often impossible. Some Southern sharecroppers became so indebted to their masters that they never saw an actual dollar bill. The money was spent long before it was earned. One sharecropper recalled the difficulty he had in trying to escape dependence on the landowner. "He not gonna show me the book," he recalled. "He egvance me food and some clothes, but I don't know how much he charged me for um. I gotta take his word that I owe what he say."

In addition to using debt to limit the freedoms of black croppers, white planters curtailed the freedoms of African-Americans with local ordinances. They passed antienticement laws which forbade attempts by landowners to lure laborers out of preexisting contracts, enacted vagrancy laws to curtail the ability of the unemployed to travel even to find work, and used the region's credit system to secure the dependency of sharecroppers. Newly emancipated blacks may have wanted to escape the world of the Southern plantations, but this was not easily done. On the eve of World War I, most African-Americans lived close to the way they had during slavery.

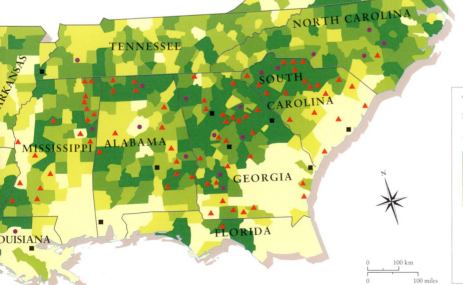

The crop-lien system, 1880

Farms sharecropped by county, in percent

- 81.0
- 34.2
- 25.8
- 19.6
- 12.7
- 0

■ commercial center

● urban cotton center

▲ rural cotton center

0   100 km

0   100 miles

VIRGINIA

NORTH CAROLINA

TENNESSEE

ARKANSAS

SOUTH CAROLINA

MISSISSIPPI   ALABAMA

GEORGIA

LOUISIANA

FLORIDA

The Praying South

Among the first segregated institutions in the postwar South were its churches. In the wake of emancipation, African-Americans established their own churches as a sign of their newfound freedom, while many white Southerners shut blacks out of their once integrated religious institutions. In the following years, the segregated Southern churches expanded and multiplied. Through newspapers and revivals, African-American ministers spread the gospel and raised money to build church buildings throughout the region. The messages of salvation and redemption were well received by many previously unchurched black Southerners. By 1890, the African Methodist Episcopal and African Methodist Episcopal Zion churches claimed over three hundred thousand members each. At the same time, over 1.3 million African-Americans attended Baptist churches in the South. Over a quarter of a million others were practicing Presbyterians or Methodists. During the postwar years, African-American churches became some of the largest institutions in many Southern cities. White churches were equally powerful. With the sole exception of Louisiana, every Southern state contained a Protestant majority, with over ninety percent of all churchgoers east of the Mississippi River attending evangelical Baptist or Methodist churches.

Other religious denominations were not shut out of the New South. Catholics, Episcopals, Lutherans, Quakers, Jews, and other religious groups created vibrant local communities, even as the evangelical movements proliferated. Catholics maintained strong followings in Louisiana and the Gulf Coast, and a theological range of religions permeated the Piedmont. In places where the Baptists monopolized the religious practices, religious communities often divided themselves with theological rationales that were not fathomable to those outside the community. One Baptist church in Tennessee watched some of its members

Black and white Methodists and Baptists, 1926

Proportion of blacks in adult population, in percent

52
40
35
20
7

Proportion of total adult population in Baptist and Methodist Churches, in percent

20 — white
10 — black
0

leave and establish a rival church when a dispute over installing a coat peg caused an irreconcilable division.

During the postwar era, more Southerners became involved in formal religious institutions than ever before. Southerners—white and black—were less churched than other Americans at the end of Reconstruction. With antebellum farms scattered throughout the countryside, church memberships were hard to maintain and churches themselves difficult to finance. Most churches hired absentee pastors and could afford to hold only monthly services. Developments after Reconstruction helped churches spread their influence. Urbanization provided the critical mass of people in certain areas to allow Southern churches to grow. All but two Southern states had their church memberships grow faster than their populations after the Civil War. Many of these evangelical churches evidenced a particular style of religion that merged intense emotionalism with biblical literalism. John Broadus, himself a Northern Baptist preacher, could not approve of the passionate sermons he witnessed in the South. "It is a common fault" he complained of the Southern ministers "to bring down the hand with a slap on the thigh, a movement necessarily ungraceful, or to slap the hands frequently together, which is very rarely appropriate; and some preachers have quite a time of banging the Bible." Not surprisingly, Broadus was equally dismayed by the intense emotionalism within the congregation. The Bible-thumping of Southern ministers was matched by the spontaneous screams and songs of the previously unchurched assembly.

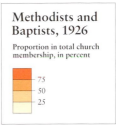

Methodists and Baptists, 1926

Proportion in total church membership, in percent

- 75
- 50
- 25

Southern churches—like churches elsewhere—fulfilled a wide range of functions. Churches obviously addressed the spiritual and theological concerns of their constituents, but their appeal also resulted from their ability to address economic, educational, cultural, recreational, and social needs. In the New South, these functions were often more important than the theological differences between the denominations. Churches provided their communities with Sunday schools, picnics, community meals, baseball games, moral instruction, "all-day sings," revivals, and other forms of religiously acceptable entertainment. Perhaps most important, the church became a place for social gatherings. As one white Mississippi resident wrote in the 1890s, the church was "the only place where people met regularly and visited with each other. Almost everyone would arrive at the church early in order to talk to the neighbors." Teenage boys and girls met each other at churches, and, under the supervision of the entire adult community, many relationships began in reserved "courting sections." In essence, the church became a place where Southerners could "hear the news" about God and about their neighbors.

Lynching and the New Racial Order

The Ku Klux Klan and similar organizations threatened the new legal rights of the freed black population, effectively denying access to the ballot box and education. Their methods are attacked in this political cartoon.

The withdrawal of Federal troops in 1877 allowed Southern whites to create a regional code of behavior that would persist far into the twentieth century. At the heart of this new code was the rejection of the economic, cultural, and political rights recently granted to freed African-American slaves which was known as Jim Crow. The Jim Crow system eliminated the participation of African-Americans in the political and legal spheres—as voters, office holders, jurists, and citizens. Grandfather clauses, literacy tests, and understanding clauses all created barriers to keep the freedmen from voting and legally reserved most of these political rights for Southern whites. Over the following decades, places across the South segregated countless public accommodations—including restrooms, restaurants, trains, and water fountains. Southerners—white and black—obeyed the standards of behavior or paid the consequences. Most of these rules went unstated and were rigorously enforced by acts of extralegal violence. The Ku Klux Klan, other paramilitary groups, and informal community mobs used lynching to enforce the unstated racial rules of behavior. Between 1882 and 1968, lynchers took the lives of over 3,400 blacks and 1,300 whites between 1882 and 1968. The last two decades of the nineteenth century were the deadliest. In 1892 at least 235 Southern blacks were killed. The maintenance of "law and order" dictated countless other acts of intimidation.

Lynching was not unique to the New South. It began in seventeenth-century Ireland, was transported to eighteenth-century North America, and flourished along the frontier beyond the reach of formal law. Revolutionary mobs assaulted Loyalists during the War of Independence, and in the following decades, abolitionists, Catholics, immigrants, and African-Americans all faced the violence and threats of violence of Northern urban mobs. By the late nineteenth and early twentieth centuries, however, lynching became nearly exclusive to the New South. Mob violence typically ignored and offended community standards of behavior. In the South, however, prominent members of the communities participated in the mob actions, including sheriffs, mayors, and ministers, and mobs occasionally worked with the consent and encouragement of the larger community. While Northern newspapers and magazines condemned the murders, their Southern counterparts issued defenses of lynching. Lynching became a Southern ritual that worked alongside local legal structures to enforce and create communal standards.

Lynchings occurred in some Southern regions more than others. The Gulf Plain that extended from Florida to Texas and the Cotton Belt of Mississippi, Arkansas, Louisiana, and Texas had the most incidents. In part, the high incidence of lynching in these areas resulted from the shared white experience of coping with a large influx of black migrants during the late nineteenth century. The arrival of African-American newcomers aroused the fear and uncertainty of local white residents, who responded with violence. The migrants also suffered from a lack of protection from white employers who could vouch for their reputations when accused and punished by lynch mobs.

Lynchings were gruesome. Before the mobs executed their victims, they typically held an informal trial. In this venue, victims faced false accusations of every crime imaginable—theft, arrogance, murder, impolite stares, intransigence, vagrancy, and rape. After presenting evidence of a supposed crime, the mobs used brutal beatings to obtain confessions and then served as juries to determine the fate of the victim. Then came hours of painful torture. Accused blacks were burned, dragged, hanged, shot, or stabbed, or some combination of these.

By the late nineteenth century, Southern white men had formally entrenched the myth of the rape complex. Although Southerners frequently justified lynch law and mob rule as necessary for the protection of white women's virtue, only one in six lynch mobs even alleged that they were avenging the rape of a white woman by a black man. In the 1890s, African-American journalist Ida B. Wells publicized this misconception. Later, during the Great Depression, the Atlanta-based Association of Southern Women for the Prevention of Lynching, an organization of mostly upper-class white women, reiterated Wells's claims and further argued that such a justification actually hurt Southern white women. Regardless of claims to the contrary, throughout lynching's heyday white Southerners justified the ritual as a defense of white female purity and honor. Despite federal laws designed to protect Southern blacks, few participants in lynchings were ever convicted in the South for the murder of black men. In fact, the first successful federal conviction for a lynching occurred in 1898 in response to the murder of two Seminole Indian teenagers in Maud, Oklahoma.

A decline in New South lynching occurred in the late 1920s. In 1953, for the first time, no lynching occured in the United States The antilynching campaigns and an altered regional economy led to the decline of the traditional form of law and order.

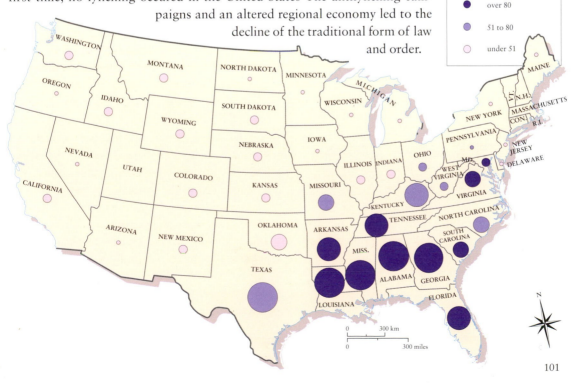

Lynching, by state, 1889–1918

Number of lynchings by state

- 251 to 386
- 141 to 250
- 41 to 140
- 11 to 40
- 1 to 10

Proportion of blacks in lynchings, in percent

- over 80
- 51 to 80
- under 51

The Great Migration

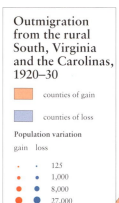

Outmigration from the rural South, Virginia and the Carolinas, 1920–30

- counties of gain
- counties of loss

Population variation

gain   loss

- 125
- 1,000
- 8,000
- 27,000
- 64,000

VIRGINIA

Richmond

Greensboro

NORTH CAROLINA

Charlotte
Greenville

SOUTH CAROLINA

N

0 ___ 100 km
0 ___ 100 miles

After finding work in a Chicago packing plant, a recent African-American migrant wrote to friends he left behind in the South. "The people are rushing here by the thousands and I know if you come and rent a big house you can get all the roomers you want. You write me exactly when you are coming. I am not keeping house yet I am living with my brother and his wife. . . . I can get a nice place for you to stop until you can look around and see what you want." His optimism could not be overstated. "I feel like God made the path and I am walking therein."

At the turn of the century, hundreds of thousands of African-American Southerners shared this belief that Northern cities were promised lands: divine refuges from the racism and limited economic opportunities inherent to the South. During World War I, over 400,000 acted on their inner convictions and left their predominantly rural Southern homes for Northern and Midwestern cities. The Southern countryside did not quite empty, but the exodus certainly left its mark on the landscape. In Mississippi alone, nearly 100,000 African-American migrants left for the paved pastures of the urban landscape. At the same time, the black populations of every major Northern city multiplied. In the 1910s, Chicago's black population increased 148 percent, Cleveland's over 300 percent, and Detroit's an astronomical 611 percent. In 1920, nearly forty percent of all African-Americans in the North lived in eight cities: New York, Philadelphia, Pittsburgh, Chicago, Detroit, Cleveland, Cincinnati, and Columbus, Ohio. Other lesser known areas were equally affected. Richmond, California, for example, went from a town with twenty-nine black residents in 1910 to one with over one hundred thousand at the end of World War II. This "Great Migration" changed the racial landscape of the entire nation.

The desire of many African-Americans to the leave the South extended back to the days of slavery. When freedom did not prove the panacea they had hoped for, many blacks wanted to leave the South to escape its disfranchisement, segregation, legal inequality, police mistreatment, verbal abuse by neighboring whites, lynchings, limited opportunities for education, and racial subordination. A series of crop failures due to the boll weevil early in the century made a migration North even more desirable. The migration, however, was initiated more by the positive attractions of the

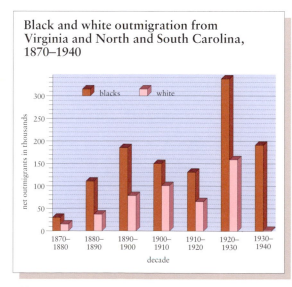

Black and white outmigration from Virginia and North and South Carolina, 1870–1940

net outmigrants in thousands

blacks   white

300
250
200
150
100
50
0

1870– 1880– 1890– 1900– 1910– 1920– 1930–
1880 1890 1900 1910 1920 1930 1940

decade

North than the negative realities of the South. World War I—its demands for industrial goods, the associated decline in European immigration, and the military's enlistment of thousands of workers—created an abundance of jobs in many Northern cities. Factory owners could often not afford to use their traditional and discriminatory hiring practices. Jobs that African-Americans were once prohibited from performing became available during the war. The labor shortage was so severe that some Northern industries actively recruited black workers. Armed with railroad passes provided by factory owners, and the belief that they could find work, black families migrated toward these opportunities. Northern black newspapers, most notably the Chicago *Defender*, recounted the success stories of earlier migrants and announced the opportunities that could be found in the cities.

Those who fled the South did not detach themselves from family and friends. In many cases, entire families or the majority of church congregations moved as a group. Many black community leaders—ministers, politicians, and businessmen—tried to stop the outmigration of supporters. Those who lost the fight frequently uprooted themselves and followed their parishioners, constituents, and clients. Other Southern blacks migrated as individuals, only to encourage their friends, relatives, and neighbors to join them in the months and years that followed. Although many black migrants came to recognize the racial and economic shortcomings of their new communities, the limited opportunities of the North remained a powerful draw.

Commemorating the African-American migration northward, this 1940s painting by Jacob Lawrence is entitled The Migration of the Negro.

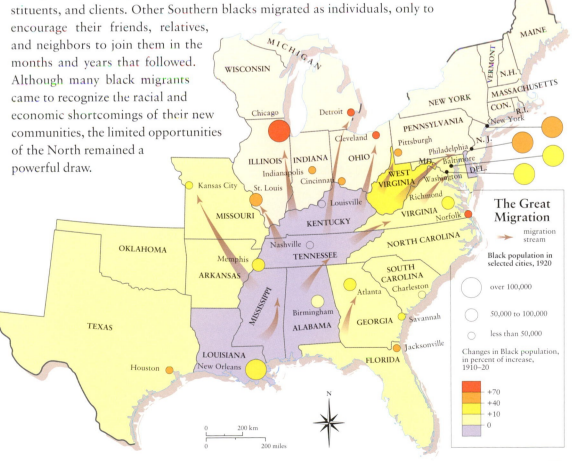

The Great Migration

→ migration stream

Black population in selected cities, 1920

○ over 100,000

○ 50,000 to 100,000

○ less than 50,000

Changes in Black population, in percent of increase, 1910–20

+70
+40
+10
0

0 ___ 200 km
0 ___ 200 miles

Southern Conservatism and the Monkey Trial

In 1925, the nation's attention focused on Dayton, Tennessee, a town of two thousand residents. Dayton officials charged John Thomas Scopes, a twenty-four-year-old high school science instructor, with teaching evolution in defiance of a state law. Tennessee's recently enacted Butler Act made it "unlawful . . . to teach any theory that denies the story of the Divine Creation of man as taught in the Bible, and to teach instead that man has descended from a lower order of animals." Upon the law's enactment, the American Civil Liberties Union had declared that they would pay for the legal services of anyone accused of breaking the law, and Scopes quite unintentionally became that person. Scopes proclaimed his innocence. Not only did he believe that Darwinian evolution and the Bible could be reconciled, but he also used a state-adopted textbook which contained a discussion of evolution to teach his class. This did not satisfy Scopes's opponents, and a well-publicized trial ensued.

Clarence Darrow, a vocal agnostic and renowned attorney from Chicago, signed on as Scopes's attorney and defended his right to teach evolution. On the other side, William Jennings Bryan, former Populist and presidential candidate, took up the prosecution. The nation's reporters came to see what became known as the "Monkey Trial." Darrow outdueled Bryan, finding contradictions in the state's case and pointing to parts of the Bible that even Bryan would not take literally. Although he was outmatched in legal machinations, Bryan's presentation of the basic facts brought a conviction and a hundred-dollar fine for Scopes. Soon after the *Baltimore Sun* paid the fine, the Supreme Court of Tennessee overturned the verdict on a technicality.

The Scopes Monkey Trial, although blown out of proportion by the national media attention, displayed the conservative nature of Southern society in the late nineteenth and early twentieth centuries. Indeed, few Northern

Socialist activities
in cities and towns, 1911–20

●   Socialist mayors or municipal officers
     elected, 1911–20

▪   Socialist periodicals published, 1912–18

journalists learned anything new about the
South when they came to Dayton to cover the
trial. Quite the contrary, most simply confirmed their
preconceptions. H. L. Menken, a columnist from
Baltimore, had long perceived the South to be the undeveloped land of ignorance and prejudice. "In that whole region," Menken wrote "an area three
times as large as either France or Germany, there is not a single symphony
orchestra, nor a single picture worth looking at, nor a single public building or
monument of the first rank, nor a single factory devoted to the making of
beautiful things, nor a single poet, novelist, historian, musician, painter or
sculptor whose reputation extends beyond his own country." For Menken, the
trial was simply a source of more colorful evidence. "The thing is genuinely
fabulous" Menken wrote of the trial. "I have . . . enough material stored up to

Homicides and executions, by state, 1930s

Number of homicides per million inhabitants, per year, 1938–39

- 278
- 200
- 100
- 60
- 44
- 26
- 2

Average number of executions, per year, 1930–34

⚱ 1 execution

Mode of executions, 1939

✦ electrocution

✦ hanging

✦ gassing

✦ shooting

last me the rest of my life." Indeed, Menken left the trial before it ended and returned to Baltimore, where he continued to present critical portrayals of the South.

Although Menken misunderstood as much as he understood about the South, he provided keen insight into the many ways in which the South was a closed and conservative society. Although progressive reformers had some successes in the South, many national reforms faced stiff resistance in the South. The push for women's suffrage, for example, had its hardest time in the southeast. The Nineteenth Amendment—which gave women the vote— was slowly, and sometimes only reluctantly, accepted in the South. Some Southern whites feared that expanding suffrage would upset the system of disfranchisement that prevented African-Americans from voting, while others rejected the idea of a capable female electorate. When the necessary three quarters of the states ratified the amendment, only five supporting states were in the South. Not surprisingly, the Socialist Party of America, founded in 1901, was weakest in the region. In 1912, Eugene Debs received 12 percent of the national vote on the Socialist ticket, but could hardly obtain any Southern support outside of Texas, Arkansas, and Oklahoma. Indeed, few Southern states had any significant socialist activities during the first two decades of the twentieth century. The South elected only a handful of socialist local officials, and socialist periodicals were all but absent from the region. Progressive reformers also had difficulty eliminating capital punishment in the southeast. Southern states continued to condone state-sponsored

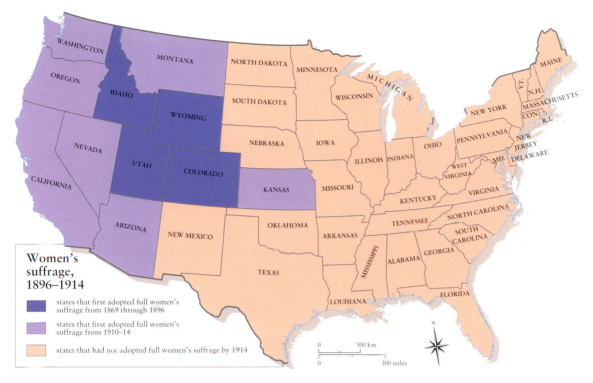

Women's suffrage, 1896–1914

- states that first adopted full women's suffrage from 1869 through 1896
- states that first adopted full women's suffrage from 1910–14
- states that had not adopted full women's suffrage by 1914

0   300 km
0   300 miles

N

executions, and they contained the highest homicide rates in the nation. As H. C. Brearley asserted in 1932, the South was "that part of the United States lying below the Smith and Wesson line."

Women's suffrage resolution May 21, 1919

- yeas
- nays
- unsettled
- not voting

0   300 km
0   300 miles

N

The Progressive Movement

After two decades of moderate changes, New South boosters could not help but recognize the shortcomings of Southern society. As the twentieth century approached, Southern states lagged far behind their Northern counterparts on almost every social and economic indicator. Southerners compared unfavorably to national averages in terms of per capita income, infant mortality, school expenditures, length of school years, and even the spread of household appliances. They had less access to electricity and thus owned fewer radios, ice boxes, and telephones. The emergence of a materialist and industrial economy created many problems—real and imagined. Progressive reformers, often middle-class women, addressed many of these sources of anxiety during the first two decades of the twentieth century.

Progressive reformers had various messages and multiple ambitions. One of their central concerns was the need to curtail the power of large corporations, especially trusts. Southerners had long complained about the undue influence of large Northern corporations and their extraction of Southern wealth. Among the most egregious centers of power were the insurance, railroad, and oil companies. One at a time, Southern states reformed these industries. By 1909, nearly every Southern state had brought some regulation to the railroads by limiting what they could charge for freight and passengers. Attacks on the other industries followed. Florida proposed that the state itself go into the insurance business to prevent the lucrative premiums from leaving the state for good. Texas, following Florida's lead, passed the Robertson Act in 1907. This law required life-insurance companies to invest a percentage of profits within Texas. Several states filed antitrust lawsuits against the oil companies.

Progressive reforms went far beyond the assault on monopolies. Municipal reform also swept through local governments. Dozens of Southern cities—

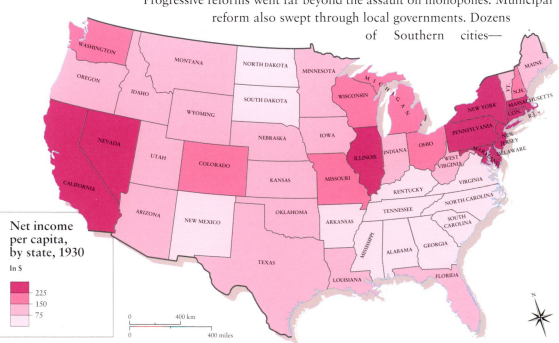

Net income per capita, by state, 1930

In $

- 225
- 150
- 75

0   400 km

0   400 miles

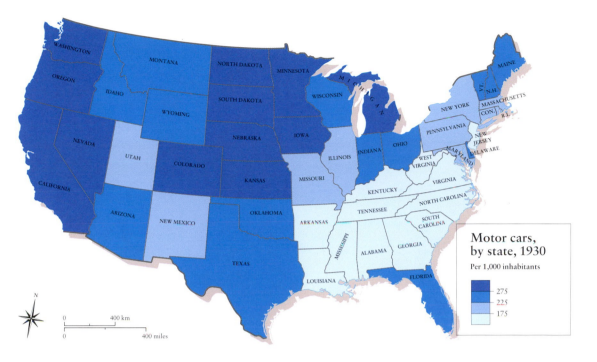

Motor cars, by state, 1930
Per 1,000 inhabitants

275
225
175

including Houston, Dallas, Memphis, New Orleans, Jackson and Birmingham—followed the lead of Galveston, Texas by adopting commission plan governments. Other Southern cities hired professional city managers. In addition, progressive laws addressed abusive child labor practices, regulated working hours and safety conditions, abolished the convict lease systems, addressed public health concerns, and created new government services to assist private businesses. Taxes necessarily needed to be raised to subsidize the new agencies. Between 1903 and 1922, Southern states increased their revenues by over four hundred percent. North Carolina, in the most dramatic change, increased its tax revenue sixfold.

Education reform received some of the most direct and overdue attention. In 1900, per-pupil expenditures in the South fell well short of the national average of $2.84. Alabama and North Carolina, for example, spent a mere fifty cents, while five other Southern states spent less than a dollar. In addition, most school-aged children in the South did not attend school and those that did attended schools that stayed open for less than four months a year. Undereducated and poorly paid, the region's teachers struggled with insufficient supplies and decrepit schoolhouses. Not surprisingly, Southern literacy rates were low. In 1900, nearly one in five white Southerners and half of black Southerners could neither read nor write. Progressive reformers addressed the problems of the region's educational system directly. State governments increased school funding while at the same time philanthropic organizations, such as the Peabody Education Fund, targeted black and white schools for assistance. By 1920, Southern states were spending $156.3 million a year on

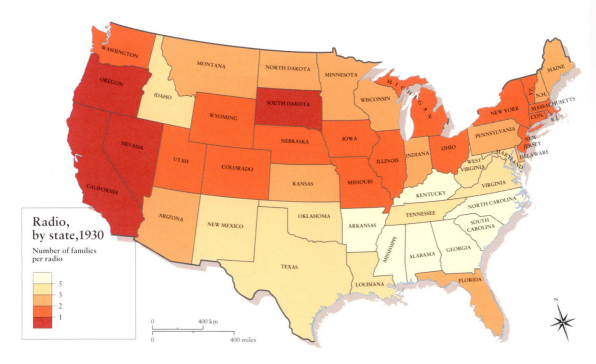

Radio, by state, 1930

Number of families per radio

- 5
- 3
- 2
- 1

0   400 km

0   400 miles

education. Only twenty years earlier, education expenditures amounted to $21.4 million. In addition to increasing financial assistance to schools, Southern states also standardized much of what was taught, enhanced the training of their teachers, relied on educational experts to design their curriculums, lengthened the school year, and looked to the region's universities for assistance. As a result of these reforms, the region's illiteracy rate was cut in half during the first decade of the twentieth century.

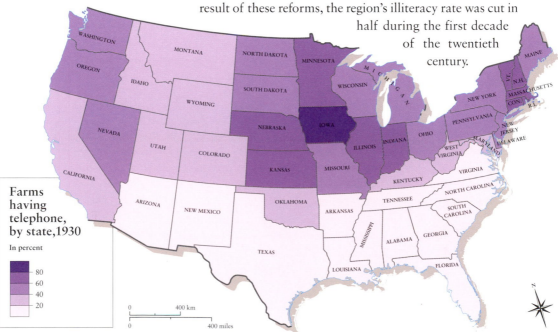

Farms having telephone, by state, 1930

In percent

- 80
- 60
- 40
- 20

0   400 km

0   400 miles

Progressive reforms did not always move the region forward. As much as progressive reformers tried to redraw the region's economic landscape, they typically maintained a status-quo approach to race relations. During the progressive era, Jim Crow laws expanded and the disfranchisement of African-Americans became complete. James Kimble Vardaman—Mississippi legislator, Governor, and then United States senator—typified the region's progressive politicians. Vardaman, who became known as the "White Chief," suggested repealing the Fifteenth Amendment and modifying the Fourteenth Amendment. Indeed, one of Vardaman's progressive ambitions was to stop all expenditures for the education of African-Americans. His rationale was clear. "Education" he asserted "only makes the Negro dissatisfied with his lowly position in society." Restoring black Southerners to their "proper place" was but one of Vardaman's so-called progressive reforms. Governor Vardaman also tried to reform the state's system of taxation, increase public expenditures on education, reform the penal system, provide services to the mentally ill, restrict child labor, and lower interest rates. Vardaman saw no contradictions in his progressive vision for the South. He could campaign against the lynching of African-Americans and encourage the legislature to pass stringent Jim Crow laws. Southern progressivism demanded both.

Racial inequality and regional poverty survived the progressive era intact. Many aspects of Southern society dramatically improved in the years prior to World War I, but the South remained the poorest region in the United States. Although Progressives restructured municipal governments and ameliorated some of the most blatant inequities in Southern society, Jim Crow and racial inequality remained entrenched as they had ever been.

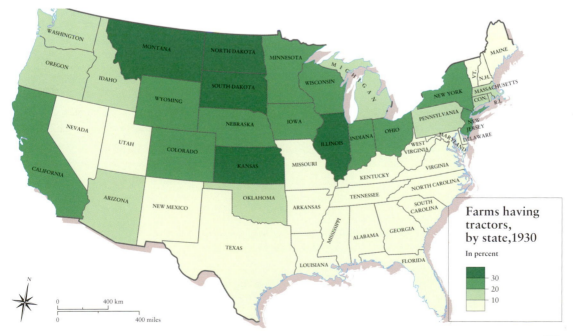

Farms having tractors, by state, 1930

In percent

30
20
10

PART V: THE MODERN SOUTH

Since Black Thursday, when the New York Stock Exchange crashed in October 1929 and the Great Depression ensued, the American South has undergone a profound transformation. Trends which had stopped short in the aftermath of Reconstruction reappeared with renewed vibrancy in the modern South. As was the case between 1865 and 1877, the federal government used its financial resources to address economic inequities within the South; African-Americans intensified their struggle for civil rights, and their concerns entered the forefront of national policy and the court systems; and the Republican Party obtained newfound allegiances in the South. Other trends which incompletely developed during the New South became full blown in the twentieth century. For example, the Southern economy modernized as the region attracted industry and businesses from across the nation; African-American leaders, who had largely struggled to have their voices heard in earlier decades, now obtained national recognition; and various commentators once again lamented, praised, and observed what they saw as the death of regionalism in America.

The modern fear that the South was on the path to disappearance had an early voice in *I'll Take My Stand*, a 1930 manifesto by twelve Southern intellectuals. Taken as a whole, their essays called for a return to an agrarian way of life and resistance to the repeated incursions of Northern society. It was, in their words, a struggle between "a Southern way of life against what may be called the American or prevailing way; and . . . the best terms in which to represent the distinction are contained in the phrase Agrarian *versus* Industrial." In recent years, these twelve Southerners have been echoed by scores of social scientists, journalists, historians, clergymen, and politicians. They have referred to "The Adaptable South," "The Disappearing South," and a "Developing Dixie." The death of regionalism and the spread of Americanism, and the corresponding perception that Southern distinctiveness was disappearing, have been attributed to various causes. For some, the region's culture was overpowered by a dominant national culture—one that has been spread by television, radio, movies, chain stores, and internal migration. The forces of modernization and federal funding have also altered the Southern landscape. As the South became more urban and industrial in the twentieth century, its rural roots have become muted. Cotton fields continue to dot the region's landscape, but now the South is interspersed with auto plants and insurance companies. New technology, even the air conditioner which made areas of the South more livable in the 1950s, has also been credited with the decline in regionalism.

In large part, the modern South has been a creation of the federal government. During the New Deal, the United States poured billions of dollars into the Southern economy. Some programs—such as the Tennessee Valley Act—addressed problems that were peculiar to the American South. Dams and waterways built by the TVA benefited the region's farmers by improving irrigation, controlling seasonal flooding, and allowing for the better navigation of the region's waterways. The TVA, along with the Rural Electrification Administration, brought electricity to areas of the rural South for the first time. Other New Deal programs addressed the national problems associated with poverty, and the impoverished South received a lion's share of federal support. The Agricultural Adjustment Act, for example, helped eliminate the overproduction that had hurt Southern farmers for generations, and it brought relative stability to the region's agricultural prices. Similarly, the Federal Emergency Relief Administration, and other agencies, loaned some Southerners the money that they needed to help survive the Depression without losing their farms, and these loans helped others purchase their own farms.

Even as federal funds continued to pour into the South after the Second World War, the national government began actively to reshape the South through legislation. Largely responses to African-American protests, a series of civil rights laws ended the disfranchisement and segregation that existed in the South. *Brown v. Board of Education of Topeka, Kansas*, the 1954 Supreme Court ruling, helped the government justify its allocation of resources to fight for racial equality. Other federal legislation, such as the Civil Rights Act of 1964 and the Voting Rights Act of 1965, helped Southern blacks overturn the pervasive system of Jim Crow segregation. In addition, the federal government used the National Guard to protect students and protesters in the 1960s and 1970s, and it provided prosecutors to enforce the newly enacted desegregation laws. The Civil Rights Movement did not solve all of the problems associated with race relations in the Modern South, but it did create a new atmosphere in which the forces of segregation and racial hostility were placed on the defensive.

In recent decades, the federal government has altered the Southern landscape through a myriad of indirect policies. Policies designed to create and improve the federal highway system as well as a dramatic increase in spending for the national defense in the post-World War II years helped create and invigorate what has become known as the Sun Belt. A geographic area that extends from Virginia to Southern California, the Sun Belt has attracted corporations and individuals to its inviting economic climates. Sun Belt cities took advantage of federal assistance as they promoted a new image of the region; the Modern South was "too busy to hate" and ideally suited for economic growth. They offered low tax rates, inexpensive labor costs, and modern infrastructures. By 1980, Sun Belt growth had reduced many of the economic disparities between the regions.

Despite all of these powerful forces in the twentieth century, the American South persisted. Modern Southerners still voted, prayed, ate, and talked differently from other Americans. Regional identities continued to shape where students attended college, whom Southerners married, how they voted, and how they perceived themselves. In other words, differences between Southerners and Northerners survived the forces of modernization, and the Modern South did not become a carbon copy of the North. Instead, elements of the Southern past have shaped its present, and the Modern South has developed into a hybrid of old and new.

The Tennessee Valley Authority

The Great Depression brought complete financial ruin to a region that had no recent memory of prosperity. Unlike the rest of the nation, the South had not enjoyed the economic boom of the 1920s. Yet the crash of the stock market on Thursday, October 24, 1929, unleashed forces that exaggerated the region's pre-existing agricultural and industrial miseries. Unemployment jumped to above twenty percent in most Southern cities, foreclosure threatened small farmers, and a drought which began in the winter of 1929 devastated the region's crops. By 1932, the per-capita income fell forty-four percent, industrial production declined by half, and bankruptcy threatened state and local governments. More than a third of all Southern banks did not survive the Depression, and when the Nashville investment firm of Caldwell and Company crashed, it nearly took the state government of Tennessee with it. Three other Southern states, Louisiana, South Carolina, and Arkansas, defaulted on their loans. Bankruptcy threatened every Southern state. In 1932, Mississippi had barely a thousand dollars in reserve and over fourteen million dollars in outstanding loans.

Nearly three and a half years after "Black Thursday," newly elected President Franklin Roosevelt began implementing his New Deal. Within the first hundred days of his administration, Roosevelt pushed fifteen acts through Congress. Roosevelt created a virtual "alphabet soup" of policies and programs—including the Emergency Banking Act (EBA), the Home Owners Loan Corporation (HOLC), the Glass-Steagall Act, the Federal Deposit Insurance Corporation (FDIC), the Civilian Conservation Corps (CCC), the Agricultural Adjustment Act (AAA), the National Recovery Administration (NRA), the Federal Emergency Relief Administration (FERA), the Public Works Administration (PWA), and the Civil Works Administration (CWA). For impoverished Southerners, the New Deal offered farming subsidies, relief from foreclosures, access to publicly funded jobs, and a regulated stock market. Congress also established the most enduring legacy in the South—the Tennessee Valley Authority (TVA).

The TVA did more than create jobs for thousands of Southerners. It literally reshaped the landscape of the seven Southern states that touched the Tennessee River—Tennessee, Alabama, Mississippi, Kentucky, Virginia, North Carolina, and Georgia. It provided government ownership of municipal services, built five dams, fixed twenty other dams, created a system of inland waterways, improved the navigation of crooked rivers, implemented plans of reforestation and soil conservation, funded fertilizer research, and affected a drainage area of over 40,569 square miles. Perhaps most impressively, the TVA along with the Rural Electrification Administration (REA) brought electricity to a region that had previously relied largely on kerosene and coal. One out of five farms in the region received electricity because of the TVA. Electricity transformed the region. "Two million kilowatts cannot be turned loose in a Valley without some shocks being felt," C. Herman Pritchett asserted.

Despite its benefits, the TVA had its critics. Dwight D. Eisenhower called it an example of "creeping socialism," while many Southerners viewed it as an intrusive government agency. Mississippi-born author William Faulkner mourned the environmental costs of the TVA. "The Big Woods, the Big Bottom, the wilderness, vanished now from where he had first known it; the very spot where . . . he heard his first running hounds and cocked his gun and saw the first buck, was now thirty feet below the surface of a government-built flood control reservoir whose bottom was rising gradually and inexorably each year on another layer of beer cans and bottle tops." During the 1930s, the voices of dissent were generally rejected for their "ignorance" and short-sightedness. Many complaints, however, were well-founded. Newly built dams, especially the Norris Dam, forced the relocation of hundreds of residents when their lands became covered with floodwaters. Electricity plants spewed the ashes of burning coal into the air, making some places unlivable. The town of Paradise, Kentucky, for example, had to be abandoned after the TVA built an electricity plant there. Although the TVA brought employment opportunities to the region, they conformed to Jim Crow standards. Local agencies, which worked with the TVA, systematically excluded African-Americans from many labor pools and segregated them into the poorest paying jobs in others.

In 1938, President Roosevelt proclaimed "It is my conviction that the South presents right now the Nation's No. 1 economic problem—the Nation's problem, not merely the South's." The TVA addressed this problem directly. Although many of its economic benefits did not become apparent until after World War II, the TVA reshaped the heartland of the South. For the first time since Reconstruction, the federal government took an active role in shaping Southern society.

The Tennessee Valley Authority

— limit of the TVA

▬ dam

▬ dam operated by Corps of Engineers

▬ dam operated by Aluminium Co. of America

◆ steam plant

Rosa Parks and the Montgomery Buses

On March 22, 1956, Reverend Martin Luther King, Jr., proclaimed "I believe that God is using Montgomery as his proving ground. It may be that here in the [first] capital of the Confederacy, the birth of the ideal of freedom in American and in the Southland can be born." Indeed, in the 1950s, Montgomery served as a vanguard for the Civil Rights Movement, as its African-American community challenged the ingrained code of Jim Crow. When King spoke these words, however, few blacks were registered to vote, the city of 120,000 had no elected black officials, and segregation permeated every aspect of society. Recent events within Montgomery's African-American community, however, provided King with an optimism that this world would be turned upside down.

By refusing to give up her seat to a white passenger, Rosa Parks became the starting point of a bus boycott and protest against the segregation law.

Four months before King's prophetic statement about the Alabama capital, a series of events brought Montgomery to the national stage. On December 1, 1955, Rosa Parks boarded the 5:30 p.m. bus outside Montgomery Fair, a department store on Dexter Avenue where she worked as a seamstress. She took her seat in one of the back rows that were available to whites or blacks. After a couple of blocks, the bus arrived at the Empire Theater bus stop, where several white men boarded the bus. The driver, realizing that there were not enough seats for the white men in the first ten rows, yelled a refrain common to the Jim Crow South, "Niggers, move back." Parks refused. The driver asked her again, and Parks who was tired from a long day of work, replied with a simple and emphatic "no."

The driver left the bus, and notified the local police, who arrested Parks and took her to jail. Parks was not the first black woman to be taken into custody for such an act of defiance on a Montgomery public bus. Similar incidents had occurred months earlier in March and October. The events after the arrest, however, elevated the importance of Parks's decision to remain seated. Three black activists, who knew Parks from her activities with the local National Association for the Advancement of Colored People, paid Parks's bail. Immediately afterward, Parks agreed to let herself become a rallying cry for the local African-American community. Her arrest would become the basis for a challenge of the segregation laws and for a citywide protest against the treatment of blacks on the public buses.

Outraged and opportunistic local African-American leaders spent the ensuing weekend planning a response. The Women's Political Council of Montgomery mimeographed 52,500 leaflets and spread the news of a one-day boycott of the city's bus system. "Another Negro woman has been arrested and thrown into jail because she refused to get up out of her seat on the bus for a white person to sit down" the leaflet asserted. "This woman's case will come up on Monday. We are, therefore, asking every Negro to stay off the buses Monday in protest of the arrest and trial." Only a handful of blacks took the buses that Monday. Most walked to work or used an informal network of car

Montgomery, Alabama

Selma to Montgomery march route, 1965

pools and taxis. The bus company lost between thirty and forty thousand fares that day. In Montgomery's City Hall, however, Parks was found guilty and fined four dollars plus court costs.

That evening, several thousand African-Americans celebrated their successful boycott and appointed King as the spokesperson for their movement. King, who had come to the Dexter Avenue Baptist Church less than a year and a half earlier, extended the boycott indefinitely. Through the Montgomery Improvement Association, King demanded that the city's bus drivers be more courteous to black riders, that passengers be seated on a first-come, first-served basis, and that more black drivers be hired to drive the predominantly black routes. When negotiations with the bus company broke down in February 1956, the boycott leaders filed their objections in court. Ten months later, on November 13, 1956, the Supreme Court declared the segregation law unconstitutional. The bus boycott ended in December.

Although Montgomery accepted the court order to desegregate the buses, the message of integration hardly permeated the white community. No black bus drivers were hired in the aftermath of the boycott, antagonism continued between white and black riders, and most public facilities remained segregated. When a federal court told Montgomery to integrate its public parks, city officials chose to close them instead. The parks would not reopen until 1965. That same year, King brought Alabama's capital back into national attention by leading a protest march from Selma to Montgomery.

The Freedom Rides

On May 4, 1961, thirteen riders, seven black and six white, boarded south-bound Greyhound and Trailways buses in Washington, DC. The riders were determined to challenge the segregation of public facilities and transportation in the Deep South. The Supreme Court had recently ruled that interstate bus systems could not segregate their facilities, but the riders knew the decision was being ignored. Organized by the Congress of Racial Equality (CORE), a biracial direct action group in the North, these Freedom Riders planned to travel through Virginia, the Carolinas, Georgia, Alabama, and Mississippi on buses. Riders would intentionally disregard the segregated rules in the terminal restaurants, waiting areas, water fountains, and restrooms. James Farmer, the founder of CORE, recalled that "Our intention was to provoke the Southern authorities into arresting us and thereby prod the Justice Department into enforcing the law of the land."

In 1947, CORE had organized the "Journey of Reconciliation" through the Upper South. The sixteen riders discovered the widespread disregard for the *Morgan v. Virginia* (1946) ruling. The protest resulted in several arrests in North Carolina when the white participants sat in the back and the black participants sat in the front of Greyhound and Trailways buses.

Unlike these earlier riders, the Freedom Riders faced little opposition in the Upper South. They rode through Virginia and North Carolina with little resistance. The trip took a different turn in Rock Hill, South Carolina. When the riders tried to enter the "whites only" waiting room, several South Carolinians violently intervened by beating John Lewis and Albert Bigelow. The police finally interceded when protesters knocked a white female CORE member to the ground. The Freedom Riders reboarded their buses and continued without incident through Athens, Augusta, and then Atlanta, Georgia.

On Sunday, the Greyhound bus reached Anniston, Alabama. There an awaiting mob immediately attacked it. The arrival of the local police provided enough time for the bus to flee the station, but not before the mob had smashed most of the windows and punctured the tires.

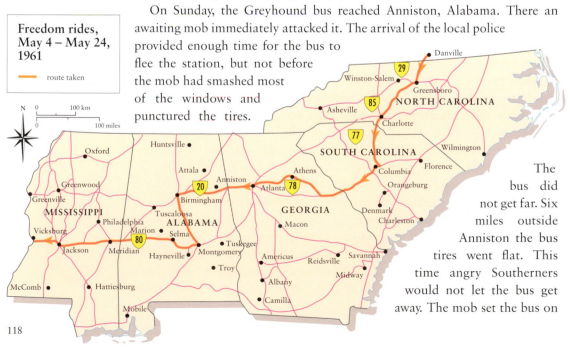

Freedom rides, May 4 – May 24, 1961

— route taken

The bus did not get far. Six miles outside Anniston the bus tires went flat. This time angry Southerners would not let the bus get away. The mob set the bus on fire, and brutally beat the passengers as they tried to escape the flames. When the Trailways bus arrived in Anniston an hour later, it too faced the wrath of an angry mob.

Later that day the Freedom Riders, now traveling together on one bus, reached the Birmingham, Alabama, Trailways station. James Peck, a white rider who had also participated in the 1946 ride, and Charles Person, a black man, got off of the bus and went to the lunch counter. Peck was quickly grabbed, and Person was dragged outside by local protesters. Local Ku Klux Klan members assaulted them with lead pipes and metal chains. They knocked Peck unconscious and also attacked several black witnesses. Police Commissioner Eugene "Bull" Connor allowed the local Klan to beat the riders for a quarter of an hour before he and his force intervened. Connor explained that the police did not immediately "save" the riders because it was Mother's Day, and his policemen were all busy visiting their mothers. A local newspaper reporter photographed the fifteen-minute attack and his pictures were carried by the Associated Press. Within days, the brutal treatment of the Freedom Riders became national news and a gloomy reminder of Jim Crow inequities.

The beatings did not play well on national television. An angered President John F. Kennedy and Attorney General Robert F. Kennedy determined to provide federal assistance to the riders. As the Kennedy brothers struggled to find a solution to the violence, the original Freedom Riders took the last leg of their journey, from Birmingham to New Orleans, by plane. On May 17, the battered Freedom Riders attended a rally that marked the seventh anniversary of the *Brown v. Board of Education* ruling.

Within three days, the Freedom Ride continued without the original riders. Twenty-one members of the Student Nonviolent Coordinating Committee (SNCC) from Nashville and Atlanta finished the bus trip to New Orleans. On May 20, they arrived in Montgomery, where the events of earlier days were repeated. Once again the riders faced an angry and violent mob, this time numbering over one thousand. One Justice Department official telephoned Robert Kennedy to describe the horrific scene. "The Passengers are coming off, a bunch of men led by a guy with a bleeding face are beating them. There are no cops. It's terrible. It's terrible. There's not a cop in sight. People are yelling. 'Get'em, get'em' It's awful." The assault led Kennedy to call for a "cooling off period" but strengthened the resolve of the riders to continue. On May 24, twenty-seven Freedom Riders left Montgomery for Jackson, Mississippi. The Mississippi National Guard escorted them along their short journey. When they arrived in Jackson, the riders were almost immediately arrested.

The Freedom Ride Coordinating Committee organized dozens of subsequent rides during the following months. The committee taught its participants the weapon of nonviolent direct action. By the end of the summer of 1961, more than a thousand riders had participated. Although the later rides received less attention than the first one, they too helped end segregation in interstate travel.

Voting Rights

Matin Luther King with colleagues on a protest march, Montgomery, Alabama, March 1965.

Early in the 1960s, the emphasis of the Civil Rights Movement turned from desegregating public facilities to enforcing universal suffrage. On the heels of the 1964 Civil Rights Act, which outlawed segregated public facilities and racial discrimination in employment and education, thousands of volunteers traveled to Mississippi to participate in the Freedom Summer. The volunteers established schools for black children, initiated black voter registration drives, and created the Mississippi Freedom Democratic Party (MFDP) as an alternative to the all-white Democratic party in Mississippi. The assault on the entrenched political power of white Mississippians faced resistance. Fifteen civil rights workers were brutally murdered that summer, and little more than a thousand new voters were registered. The MFDP obtained favorable national attention, but it failed to claim the seats of the Mississippi delegation to the 1964 National Democratic Convention.

Several barriers prevented most African-Americans from voting in the years preceding 1964. In many areas, registration procedures along with economic and physical intimidation limited voter registration. Registering to vote or organizing a voter's registration drive attracted the attention of local Ku Klux Klan members as well as retribution by many white employers. Poll taxes and literacy tests also prevented poor and uneducated blacks from voting.

In February, 1965, white Alabamans murdered Jimmy Lee Jackson, a black voting right's activist. In response, Martin Luther King, Jr., and other black leaders organized a massive march from Selma, Alabama, to the state capital in Montgomery. Their March 7 protest was immediately met by mounted state troopers as they tried to cross the Alabama River on Edmund Pettus Bridge just outside Selma. Images of peaceful marchers being beaten with clubs and bombarded with tear gas greeted the national television audience that evening. "Bloody Sunday," as it quickly became called, attracted hundreds of new civil rights workers to Selma. Two days later, King stopped another march before it turned bloody when local police blocked the bridge again. Later that evening, Reverend James Reeb, a Northern white minister and voting rights protester, was murdered in Selma. National outrage grew, and, within a week, President Lyndon B. Johnson ordered a joint session of Congress to respond to the situation in the South. "Their cause must be our cause too," the President stated.

"Because it is not just Negroes, but really it is all of us who must overcome the crippling legacy of bigotry and injustice. And we *shall* overcome." Johnson also warned Alabama Governor George Wallace that the march from Selma to Montgomery would proceed with the protection of the national guard. Some 25,000 marchers made the walk on March 25, 1965.

Congress passed the Voting Rights Act of 1965 on

Voting Rights Act examiners, August 1965 – August 1967

counties to which the Justice Department sent federal examiners of Voting Rights Acts

N

Little Rock
Nashville
TENNESSEE
Memphis
ARKANSAS

Richmond
VIRGINIA
Norfolk
Durham
NORTH CAROLINA
SOUTH CAROLINA
Wilington
Atlanta
Augusta
Charleston
Savannah

Dallas
TEXAS
Austin
Houston
New Orleans
LOUISIANA
MISSISSIPPI
ALABAMA
GEORGIA
Birmingham
Jackson
FLORIDA

0   200 km
0   200 miles

August 6. It prohibited literacy tests and other methods of preventing blacks from voting, created a formula to determine when the Attorney General of the United States needed to send officials to regions to register voters, and mandated that suspect counties obtain the approval of the Justice Department when they changed election procedures. The Voting Rights Act did not immediately alter voting patterns in the South. When the Justice Department investigated the region's registration of black voters, it discovered a geographic pattern of defiance. Only a handful of metropolitan areas erected barriers to black voters. Similarly, rural counties with few small black communities made little attempt to prevent blacks from voting. Resistance—violent and otherwise—occurred in the rural areas where African-Americans comprised more than half of the total population. James Farmer, a member of CORE, understood the geography of resistance. "In the cities, there was an absence of the kind of repression that existed in rural areas and our activities in the cities would have primarily centered around fighting apathy. . . . But in the rural areas we knew that the fear of the sheriff and the Ku Klux Klan, together with the desire of the whites to hold onto their power by any means, would surface." In 1967, under the auspices of the Voting Rights Act of 1965, the national government sent federal agents into sixty-two counties to register black voters. Nearly all were rural regions of Alabama, Mississippi, and Louisiana. Jefferson County, Alabama, which contained Birmingham, and Hinds County, Mississippi, which contained Jackson, were the notable exceptions.

Eventually, the Voting Rights Act dramatically altered the political landscape of the South. In the 1960 only twenty percent of eligible blacks had been registered to vote in the South. This rose to thirty-nine percent in 1964 and sixty-two percent in 1971. Even Mississippi experienced a dramatic reversal. Where only eight percent of the eligible black voters registered, by 1968, over forty-four percent now voted.

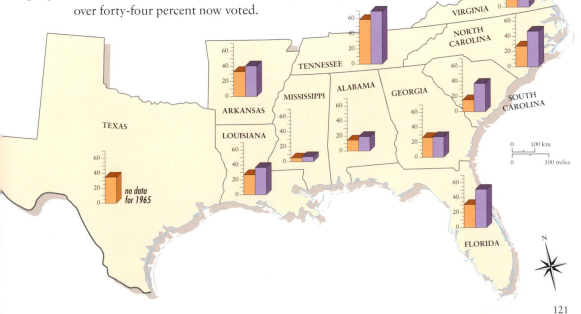

Black voter registration, 1958, 1965

proportion of black voters in nonwhite voting-age population, in percent

From Rust Belt to Sun Belt

In the decades after World War II, Henry Grady's vision of the New South finally approached reality. The Southern rim of the United States, an arc that stretches from Virginia to southern California, became the nation's fastest growing region. The "Sun Belt," as it eventually became known, experienced a 112 percent population increase in the forty years after 1940. In contrast, the population of the so-called "Rust Belt" or "Frost Belt" of the Midwest and northeast increased by forty-one percent. Northern and Eastern migrants abandoned stagnating economies, rising crime rates, and brutal winters. For the first time since the influx of carpetbaggers of Reconstruction, thousands of Northerners migrated southward. This time, they filled Southern and south-western cities such as Albuquerque, Atlanta, Dallas, Fort Worth, Houston, Los Angeles, Miami, New Orleans, Oklahoma City, Phoenix, San Antonio, San Diego, and Tampa. With favorable climates—for both business and pleasure—these cities and their environs attracted countless corporations away from the traditional urban centers of the northeast.

The economic emergence of the Sun Belt, an area of the United States which is often defined as below the 37th parallel, resulted from several forces. Perhaps most important, the federal government helped fund the Sun Belt's growth through wartime and Cold War defense spending. The government spent more than seven billion dollars on military bases and industrial plants in the South during World War II. When the war ended, navy ship-builders remained in the port cities of Mobile, Tampa, and San Diego. Inland cities throughout the Sun Belt prospered with the construction and testing of airplanes. The airplane companies, Lockheed and General Dynamic, remained in the South after the war, and they continued

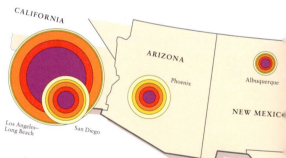

to produce military aircraft in the factories that were built in Atlanta and Fort Worth during the war. The military-industrial complex benefited the entire nation, but as one political consultant stated, the Pentagon became "a five-sided building that faces South."

The Sun Belt was not built on defense spending alone. Federal funds came southward through several other channels. The federal government financed the construction of the interstate highway system precisely at the moment that the Sun Belt cities began to burgeon. These highways brought business and travelers southbound. Not surprisingly, most Sun Belt cities built themselves up with the world of automobiles, freeways, and shopping malls in mind. In addition, federally funded urban redevelopment plans helped the Sun Belt build new stadiums, downtown civil centers, and modern airports. Social security also assisted in Sun Belt growth, as it allowed the elderly to retire to Florida, Arizona, and California in record numbers.

Sun Belt cities also provided Northern corporations and individuals with good reasons to move. These areas had low tax rates, inexpensive land and construction costs, and modern infrastructures. Some Sun Belt cities actively made themselves attractive to prospective corporations through tax rebates, highway construction, loose labor regulations, technical schools, environmental loopholes, and right-to-work laws. Finally, the Sun Belt promised newcomers an improved standard of living. Although wages normally remained lower than those in the North, the Sun Belt offered lower costs of living and the intangible qualities of "fun" and "sun." Sun Belt states improved their universities, attracted major league sports franchises, built theaters, and funded symphonies. Furthermore, the introduction of the air conditioner in the 1950s and its spread in the following decades made the Sun Belt's climate a year-round attraction.

After World War II, Southern cities prospered. The income gap between the regions declined dramatically, and in real per-capita income, Sun Belt states reached national parity in 1975. In the following years, several newspapers and magazines proclaimed that the racial antagonism of the past had disappeared. Sun Belt cities, they wrote, were "too busy to hate." Much was new in the Sun Belt, but these changes brought new challenges. Water shortages, air pollution, automobile traffic, urban sprawl, and violent

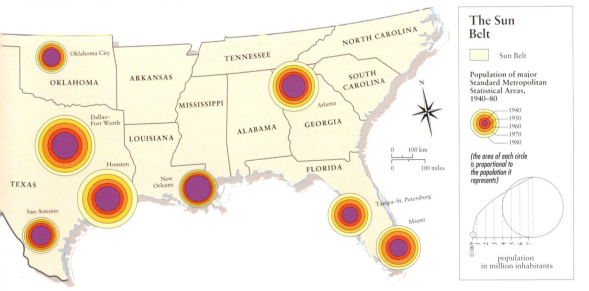

The Sun Belt

☐ Sun Belt

Population of major Standard Metropolitan Statistical Areas, 1940–80

1940
1950
1960
1970
1980

(the area of each circle is proportional to the population it represents)

0.069
1 2 3 4 5 6 7
population in million inhabitants

crime have all plagued the modern cities of the South. Continued racial antagonisms between whites, blacks, and Hispanics have also taken some of the glitter off the Sun Belt facade. The Sun Belt still attracts Northern businesses and residents and in the process is facing the problems borne of urbanization and modernization.

The Demise of the Solid South

The disfranchisement of Southern blacks and the death of the Populist Party in 1896 created a virtually unopposed Democratic Party in the South. Voices of dissent emerged five decades later when President Harry Truman desegregated the military and created a Presidential Committee on Civil Rights. Still, no viable alternative to the Democratic Party existed in the South. Alienated Southerners opposed Truman in 1948 with a Dixiecrat ticket of South Carolina Governor Strom Thurmond and Mississippi Governor Fielding Wright. In most Southern states, this ticket officially ran as that of the Democratic Party, and it carried South Carolina, Alabama, Mississippi, and Louisiana. Southerners were divided politically but remained attached to the Democratic Party. When the Civil Rights Movement destroyed the Southern system of Jim Crow during the following decade, the solidly Democratic South disintegrated.

The "Solid South" collapsed in 1964. In that year's presidential election, Texan Lyndon Johnson received the majority of the region's, and for that matter the nation's, support. He had endorsements from the Democratic parties in several states and the overwhelming support of the region's African-American voters. Yet Johnson also faced strong opposition in the South. Right-wing Republicans rallied around the conservative policies of Barry Goldwater. An advocate of state's rights and an opponent of civil rights legislation, Goldwater received the support of many alienated white Southerners. His opposition to the *Brown* decision and his vote against the Civil Rights Act of 1964 earned him the support of former Democratic voters and leaders. Alabama Governor George Wallace opposed Johnson in several primaries before he urged disillusioned white Southerners to support Goldwater. Thurmond, who was serving as a Democratic senator, changed his party allegiance and began calling himself a "Goldwater Republican." Although Goldwater lost the election, he carried five Lower South states and fifty-five percent of all Southern white voters, including a resounding eighty-seven percent of the Mississippi vote and seventy percent of the Alabama vote. Goldwater's criticism of the Tennessee Valley Authority hurt him, as did his urging of an intensification of the war in Vietnam and his hope of abandoning government services such as social security and farm subsidies. Still, the Republican Party had not enjoyed so much success in the South since Reconstruction.

National events following Johnson's 1964 reelection furthered the alienation of many white Southerners from their traditional Democratic allegiance. The Voting Rights Act of 1965 and Johnson's War on Poverty pushed white Southerners away from their Democratic base. The alienation of many Americans from the Democratic Party was compounded by antiwar protesters and by dozens of race riots, most notably in the black community of Watts near Los Angeles. By 1966, during the midyear elections, the Republican Party

Presidential elections, 1952–76

Number of times states voted Republican in 7 elections

- 6
- 5
- 4
- 3
- 2
- 1

had made strong inroads in local and state elections. It doubled its numbers within the region's state legislatures, won gubernatorial races in Arkansas and Florida, and added to its representation in the United States Congress.

In many ways, Richard Nixon followed Goldwater's path in the 1968 presidential election. Using what he called his "Southern strategy," Nixon found a powerful combination of policies to arouse the interest of white Southerners. He voiced conservative positions on national defense and expressed ideas about economic and social issues that had racial undertones. He called for less federal intervention into desegregation, criticized the policy of school busing, and promised Senator Thurmond that he would appoint a Southerner to the Supreme Court. The Southern strategy worked. Even though Wallace ran for President on a largely third-party Southern ticket, Nixon won Virginia, Tennessee, Oklahoma, Florida, North Carolina, and South Carolina. The Democratic nominee, Hubert Humphrey, won only Texas, while Wallace won all of the other Southern states. In office, Nixon turned strategy into policy. He appointed several Southerners to his administration, and in 1971 the Senate confirmed Virginian Lewis F. Powell to the Supreme Court. In 1972, the nation reelected Nixon with a Southern landslide. He won seventy-nine percent of the Southern white vote and carried every Southern state.

Since Nixon's reelection, the battle for the Southern vote has been contentious. Democrats fared poorly throughout the 1970s and 1980s in the South, and with the exception of the election of Democrat Jimmy Carter from Georgia, the party faltered nationally as well. Nixon's Southern strategy had altered the nation's political landscape, and it created a solidly Republican South. The South rallied around the party of fiscal conservatism, limited government, "law and order," opposition to affirmative action, and "traditional family values." During the 1990s, the Democratic Party has actively sought to recapture, or at least split, the South. William Jefferson Clinton, during his first run for the presidency in 1992, pursued a Southern strategy of his own. Not only did the former Arkansas Governor name a fellow Southerner as his Vice President—a "Bubba Ticket"—he mobilized moderate white voters with an agenda that had little to do with race but promised racial equality and economic improvement. Incumbent George Bush slightly outperformed Clinton in the South, but Democratic victories in Arkansas, Georgia, Louisiana, and Tennessee proved crucial to the election. The Clinton-Gore Democratic ticket won the presidency in 1992 and again in 1996.

Democrat Jimmy Carter, from Georgia, was elected President of the United States in 1976.

Presidential elections, 1980–96

Number of times states voted Republican in 5 elections

5

4

3

Missouri

Kentucky

Virginia

Oklahoma

Tennessee

North Carolina

Arkansas

South Carolina

Mississippi

Alabama

Georgia

Texas

Louisiana

Florida

0   200 km

0   200 miles

Robert E. Lee and the Modern Lost Cause

In May 1890 Richmond, Virginia, unveiled a statue of General Robert E. Lee before an audience of over one hundred thousand Southerners. The day began with a four-mile parade of school children, veteran organizations, former Confederate military units, and other honored guests. Bands played "Dixie," participants reenacted small battles, and the sounds of cannon and musket fire filled the air. Immediately after the unveiling, Archer Anderson addressed the Confederate flag and American flag waving crowd. "Let this monument, then, teach to generations yet unborn these lessons of life! Let it stand, not a record of civil strife, but as a perpetual protest against whatever is low and sordid in our public and private objects." In his address to perhaps the grandest Lost Cause festival ever, Anderson set the tone for the South's continued veneration of General Lee. Over the next century, generations "of yet unborn" white Southerners continued to portray Lee as a Southern as well as an American hero.

Richmond's celebration resembled many others in the New South. In the decades that followed Reconstruction, white Southerners erected monuments to dozens of Confederate heroes, proclaimed the continued superiority of the "Southern way," and created regional organizations such as the United Daughters of the Confederacy and the Sons of the Confederacy. Several states declared General Lee's birthday an official state holiday, and by the end of the twentieth century, dozens of Civil War memorials across the South had been erected to honor Lee. Some stood near battle sites, such as the 900-acre Lee Memorial Park near Petersburg, Virginia, while others filled prominent spaces within Southern cities such as Lexington, Mobile, New Orleans, Jacksonville, and Pensacola. Veneration of Lee was not confined to the South. Baltimore, Maryland, honored him and Thomas J. "Stonewall" Jackson with a bronze statue in its Wyman Park. The United States Military Academy at West Point, in New York, memorialized its most famous Southern graduate with Lee Gate and the Robert E. Lee Memorial Award for Excellence in Mathematics. Even today, the United States Capitol continues to house a statue of the Confederate general.

The physical reminders of the Lost Cause were not created solely in the late nineteenth and early twentieth centuries. As New South and Sun Belt development created new towns and counties, Southerners found new opportunities to continue to praise their Civil War heroes. In almost every Southern state, these opportunities meant ways to connect with General Lee. Geographic expansion and redistricting has resulted in a Lee County in nine out of the eleven Confederate States. Throughout the region, there are several towns named Leesburg, Leesburgh, Lee City, Lee's Summit, Leesville, and Lee's Crossing. Louisiana is one of the two former Confederate states without a Lee County. New Orleans, however, is crossed by Robert E. Lee Boulevard and has Lee Circle, a traffic circle with a statue of Lee in the center. Louisiana also contains counties named after Confederate General P.G.T. Beauregard and Jefferson Davis. Major roads in Louisville, Kentucky, are named Lee Avenue, Lee

Terminal, Lee Street, and Lee's Lane. Similarly, many places, including Montgomery, have a Robert E. Lee High School.

The largest monument to the Confederate past is a more recent creation. Stone Mountain, fifteen miles east of Atlanta, was dedicated to the public in 1970 and completed in 1972. The Confederate Memorial Carving is the largest relief sculpture in the world. Conceived in 1912, the project took nearly 60 years to complete. The carved figures of Lee, Confederate President Jefferson Davis, and "Stonewall" Jackson, all mounted on horseback, cover nearly three acres of the Mountain's north face. The image is 400 feet above the ground, measures 90 by 190 feet, and is recessed 42 feet into the mountain. The image of Lee on his horse Traveller is 178 feet tall. The images of the Confederate heroes survive outside a city that they could not protect from Union capture. Today, Stone Mountain attracts over four million visitors each year, a testament to the enduring power of the myth of the lost cause.

The adoration of the Confederate past promises to continue. Books on the Civil War sell disproportionately well in the South, and genealogists fill the region's libraries and archives in hopes of proving their connections to Lee and other Confederate heroes. At the same time, memberships in organizations such as the Daughters of the Confederacy and the Sons of the Confederate Veterans do not show any signs of decline. Urbanization and industrialization may have reshaped the Southern landscape, but they have not erased the region's sense of its mythical past.

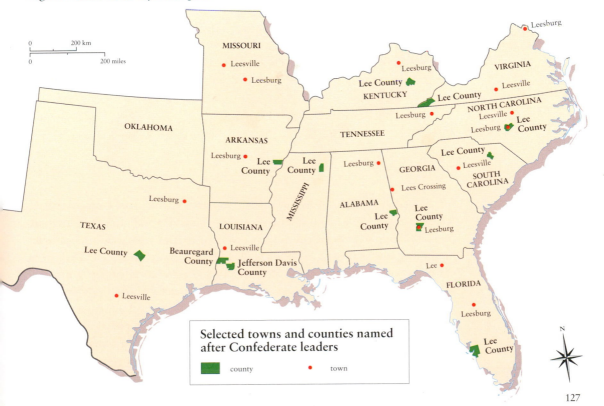

Selected towns and counties named after Confederate leaders

county • town

The End of the South?

Many critics assert that the American South is on the brink of extinction. It may continue to exist as a geographic region, they admit, but its cultural significance has all but disappeared. In addition, they argue that the Southern way of life has been radically altered by industrial progress, urban growth, the Civil Rights Movement, nationally aired television shows, and massive migrations. Today, most Southerners live in cities and work in industry. Suburban shopping malls dot the Southern landscape

Population without high school degree, by state, 1990

Proportion in population aged 25 and over, in percent

- 61.5
- 11.5
- 7.0
- 4.3
- 1.8

much as they do the rest of the nation, and immigrants from Cuba, Mexico, southeast Asia, and Jamaica have turned the biracial South into a multiethnic region. While a national culture has engulfed much of what Southerners do and think, this national culture has also become more Southern. The Great Migration brought thousands of African-Americans to Northern cities and also brought contentious racial issues to the nation as a whole. In recent years, poverty, high crime rates, and personal violence have become recognized as national shortcomings, not simply Southernisms. Sectional tensions, a mainstay in the 1950s and 1960, also seem to have subsided. Still, regionalism promises to persist deep into the twenty-first century. The South maintains a regional flavor, with its own accents, foods, music, customs, and attitudes.

Over two centuries ago, Virginian Thomas Jefferson compared the "fiery, voluptuary, indolent, [and] unsteady" Southerner with the "cool, sober, laborious, [and] independent" Northerner. In some ways, Jefferson's commentary remains true today. As much as personal violence has become a national concern in recent years, its Southern roots remain well entrenched. Southern states still have the highest homicide rates in the nation, and Southerners continue to believe more than others that violence is an acceptable form of behavior. A recent National Opinion Research Council poll revealed that two thirds of white Southern men owned guns as compared to less than half of Northern white men. In the twentieth century, Southern states have executed more criminals than the rest of the nation combined, and they participated in the first five challenges to the Supreme Court's 1972 temporary moratorium on capital punishment. In the 1990s, most convicts on death row and most executions were in Southern states. Southerners still commit more violent crime than those in the rest of the nation and these acts have a regional flavor. Whereas most homicides in the nation are impersonal or random acts, those in the South are usually personal, involving friends, families, and neighbors.

Southerners also still tend to be less educated than other Americans.

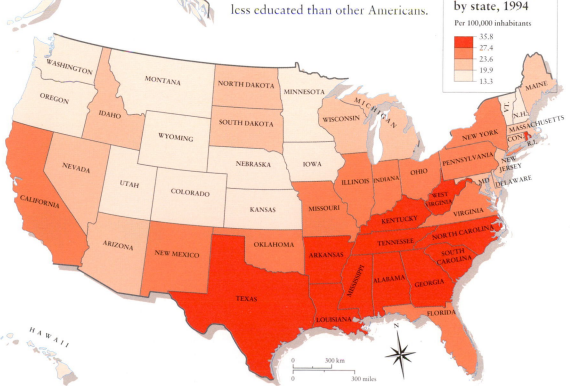

Homicide rate, by state, 1994

Per 100,000 inhabitants

	35.8
	27.4
	23.6
	19.9
	13.3

0   300 km

0   300 miles

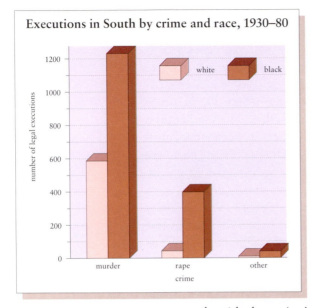

Executions in South by crime and race, 1930–80

In 1990, only nine states had more than thirty percent of its adult population lacking a high school diploma. Eight—Alabama, Arkansas, Kentucky, Louisiana, Mississippi, North Carolina, South Carolina, Tennessee—were former Confederate states. West Virginia, considered by many to be a Southern state, was the ninth. Although many Southern colleges—including Jefferson's University of Virginia—have earned national reputations for academic achievement, Southerners are also less likely to attend institutions of higher learning. Even as Southern states have increased their education expenditures to the national average, their literacy and graduation rates lag behind the rest of the nation.

The relative lack of education in the South corresponds with the region's continued economic condition. Although the Sun Belt has brought industrial growth and regional prosperity, individual Southerners remain poorer than other Americans. In 1995, eight Southern states had a higher percentage of people living below the poverty level than the national average. Only five non-Southern states accompanied Alabama, Arkansas, Florida, Kentucky, Mississippi, Missouri, Oklahoma, and Texas on this list. In recent years, per-capita income in the South has

Average annual executions, by state, 1977–93

no symbol means no execution

20 and over   10 and over   less than 10

approached national averages, but in 1990 only Florida's and Virginia's surpassed it.

Over the past century, Southern society has been undeniably altered by industrialization, urbanization, migration, and mass media. Despite the ensuing homogenization of national culture, the region continues to display distinctive traits beyond its shortcomings. Sociologist John Shelton Reed recently observed that "Southerners like the South, warts and all." While Southern culture still suffers from violence, academic underachieving, and economic shortcomings, the region continues to grow and prosper. The traits that fostered the rise of the Sun Belt—low taxes and a probusiness environment—continue to characterize the region. The South remains linked to an intangible and desirable lifestyle, one that includes neighborly hospitality, a delightful cuisine, and a mild climate. The region continues to enjoy a relatively low cost of living, its politicians have obtained national prominence, and the nation's elderly now often see the South as a desirable place to retire. Americans of all ages increasingly move to Southern towns rather than flee from them. These mixed messages of the South—like its simultaneous celebrations of the Civil War and Civil Rights—assure us that reports of the region's demise are greatly exaggerated.

Population below poverty level, by state, 1995

Proportion in total population, in percent

- 25.4
- 15.8
- 12.1
- 10.2
- 5.0

"Dixie on My Mind"

In 1917, Baltimore journalist H. L. Mencken proclaimed that the South was "almost as sterile, artistically, intellectually, culturally, as the Sahara Desert." In the decades that followed Mencken's harsh judgments, the region experienced a literary renaissance. This outpouring of creativity continued as further generations of writers brought traditionally Southern themes to a national readership. During this same period, Southern musicians regularly introduced new styles and sounds to the national and international scene.

In the twentieth century, Southern writers have prolifically contributed to the national literary canon. Many Southern authors, including, for example, Walker Percy, Flannery O'Connor, Allen Tate, and William Faulkner, depend on their Southern backgrounds for themes, characters, and plots. These authors write about Southern poverty, racism, agrarianism, and the ambiguities of progress. In addition, many white Southerners express the inner tensions evoked by regional loyalty. In *Absalom, Absalom*, for example, Faulkner's Quentin Compson struggles to come to grips with his mixed feelings about the South. Despite his condemnation of the South's association with slavery and racism, he deperately insists, "I don't. I don't! I don't hate it! I don't hate it!" For many Southern-born African-American writers, including Zora Neale Hurston, Richard Wright, Alice Walker, and Maya Angelou, the region's peculiar history of racism, poverty, and violence provided opportunities for artistic expression. However, not all Southern authors solely address Southern themes. Oklahoma-born Ralph Ellison, for example, confronted national concerns in his critically acclaimed *Invisible Man*. Although William Styron's *The Confessions of Nat Turner* draws explicitly on the region's experiences with slavery, *Sophie's Choice* explores the horrors of the European Holocaust during World War II.

While the nation did not instantly embrace Southern music, it too shaped American culture. During the twentieth century, musical forms such as country, blues, jazz, rock-and-roll, zydeco, ragtime, and gospel found audiences outside of the American South. Many Southern musicians, both black and white, drew on African musical influences and ultimately became American icons. The twentieth-century South produced, among others, Elvis Presley, Louis Armstrong, Bessie Smith,

OKLAHOMA

Oklahoma City
Ralph Ellison

Tioga
Gene Autry

TEXAS

Johnny Mercer, Ray Charles, Dizzy Gillespie, John Coltrane, "Little" Richard Penniman, Patsy Cline, Hank Williams, Muddy Waters, and Johnny Cash. Even Texan Gene Autry—the prototypical image of the West for many filmgoers—rooted his music in the South and considered himself a Southerner. Although Southern music now enjoys international appeal, it is still rooted in the region. For example, Nashville, Tennessee is widely considered the capital of country music, and New Orleans, Louisiana attracts hundreds of thousands of music fans each spring with its world-acclaimed Jazz Fest.

While many Americans still associate the South primarily with NASCAR and college football, generations of authors and musicians have proved that the region is more than rodeos and rednecks. In the modern era, Southerners have shaped the nation's musical and literary character and have attracted audiences from around the globe. Rather than a cultural desert, the American South generates many of the sounds, themes, and styles now widely considered American.

Southern authors and musicians

📖 authors

♪ musician

♪♪♪ music capital

Chronology

1000 B.C. – A.D. 1400 Native Americans build earthen mounds.

1539–43 Explorer Hernando De Soto travels into the southeastern interior.

1565 Spain establishes St. Augustine in Florida.

1585 English colonists attempt to settle Roanoke on coast of North Carolina.

1607 London's Virginia Company establishes Jamestown, the first successful English colony.

1609–11 Starving times threaten Virginia.

1617 The first shipment of tobacco leaves Virginia for England.

1619 Twenty Africans arrive in Virginia.

1622 Opechancanough leads Powhatan warriors on a surprise attack of Jamestown.

1634 Lord Baltimore establishes Maryland as a refuge for English Catholics.

1660s Virginians begin the transition away from indentured servitude and toward African slavery.

1663 King Charles II grants colonial charter for South Carolina.

1676–77 Nathaniel Bacon leads rebellion against Governor William Berkeley.

1708 Blacks constitute a majority of South Carolina's non-Indian population.

1732 James Oglethorpe obtains a charter for the colony of Georgia.

1739 South Carolina slaves initiate Stono Rebellion.

1760s Regulators attempt to create order in the Carolina backcountry.

1776 British launch a failed assault on Charles Town Harbor in South Carolina.

1788 British troops capture and occupy Savannah.

1780 American General Benjamin Lincoln surrenders Charles Town.

1781 Cornwallis invades Virginia and later surrenders at Yorktown.

1783 Eli Whitney invents the cotton gin.

1794 Toussaint L'Ouverture lead's overthrow of French rule in Saint-Domingue.

1800 Virginia militia stops Gabriel Prosser's slave conspiracy.

1800s Evangelical Protestantism spreads through South.

1803 Thomas Jefferson arranges the purchase of Louisiana.

1808 The United States ends its participation in the Atlantic slave trade.

1810s Cotton cultivation spreads westward.

1811 Slaves revolt in the Point Coupée section of the Louisiana Territory.

1812 The United States declares war on Great Britain.

1814 Creek Indians attack Fort Mims and kill 250 to 275 of the fort's inhabitants. British troops enter Washington, DC. General Andrew Jackson routs Creeks at Horseshoe Bend.

1815 Andrew Jackson defeats the British at the Battle of New Orleans.

1819 Panic of 1819 nearly cuts the price of cotton in half.

1820 Missouri Compromise defines 36° 30' as dividing line between slave and free state.

1822 South Carolinians uncover Denmark Vesey slave conspiracy before it ensues.

1823 American settlers begin to arrive in Texas.

1828 Congress passes the "tariff of abominations" to the outrage of South Carolina planters.

1829 David Walker's publishes his *Appeal . . . to the Colored Citizens of the World.*

1830 Congress passes the Indian Removal Act.

1831 Nat Turner's Rebellion unfolds in Southampton County, Virginia.

1832–33 South Carolina tries to nullify the Tariff of 1832. United States responds with the Force Bill.

1836 Texas becomes an independent republic.

1829–40 The United States removes most of the southeastern Indians west of the Mississippi River.

1830s Pro-slavery defense emerges in the South.

1837 Economic Panic of 1837 results in the depression of the cotton market.

1845 United States annexes Texas and incorporates it as a slave state.

1850 Compromise of 1850 admits California as a free state, includes a stricter Fugitive Slave Act, ends the slave trade in Washington, D. C., and uses the principle of popular sovereignty in the territories.

1852 Harriet Beecher Stowe's *Uncle Tom's Cabin* becomes a best seller.

1854 Congress overturns the Missouri Compromise by using popular sovereignty in the Kansas Nebraska-Act.

1856 Kansas bleeds when 700 proslavery men sack Lawrence, Kansas. Preston Brooks canes Massachusetts Senator Charles Sumner for his "Crime Against Kansas" speech on the Senate floor. John Brown leads Pottawatomie Massacre in Kansas.

1859 John Brown leads raid at Harpers Ferry in Virginia.

1860 Abraham Lincoln wins Presidential election. South Carolina secedes from the Union.

1861 Confederate States of America forms. Fort Sumter surrenders to Confederate forces. Virginia joins

Confederacy. South wins Battle of Bull Run. Union General Benjamin Butler declares runaway slaves as "contraband of war."

1862 Confederacy enacts conscription. Federal troops occupy New Orleans. Union troops struggle in Peninsula Campaign. South wins Second Battle of Bull Run, Americans fight the bloodiest day of the Civil War at Antietam. Robert E. Lee wins battle at Fredricksburg. Lincoln issues Preliminary Emancipation Proclamation.

1863 Lincoln issues Emancipation Proclamation. Ironclads *Virginia* and the *Monitor* engage in a three-hour standoff. Confederate troops win Battle at Chancellorsville. Federal troops emerge victorious at Gettysburg and Vicksburg. United States ratifies the Thirteenth Amendment.

1864 Ulysses S. Grant faces Lee in northern Virginia. Grant marches toward Richmond. Federal troops lay siege to Petersburg. William Tecumseh Sherman captures Atlanta and begins March to the Sea.

1865 Sherman leaves Savannah and begins march through South Carolina. Lee surrenders to Grant at Appomattox Court House. Congress established Freedmen's Bureau. John Wilkes Booth assassinates Abraham Lincoln. Andrew Johnson launches Presidential Reconstruction.

1866 President Johnson vetoes Freedmen's Bureau Bill and Civil Right Act. Congress passes Fourteenth Amendment.

1866 Nathan Bedford Forrest creates Ku Klux Klan.

1867 Congress overrides presidential veto of Reconstruction Act.

1869 Fifteenth Amendment secures blacks the right to vote.

1870–71 Ku Klux Klan Acts attempt to protect black voters.

1876 Election between Republican Rutherford B. Hayes and Democrat Samuel J. Tilden results in secret compromise.

1877 Federal troops withdraw from South. Reconstruction ends.

1880s Southern states institute Jim Crow laws.

1884 James A. Bonsack invents machine that automatically rolls cigarettes.

1886 Newspaper editor Henry Grady coins term "New South Creed."

1890 Mississippi begins to use literacy tests to disfranchise its black voters.

1892 Atlanta builds the first skyscraper in the South—the Equitable Building.

1896 *Plessy v. Ferguson* upholds the constitutionality of segregated public facilities. Populism movement collapses.

1910s Hundreds of thousands of African-Americans embark on a Great Migration out of the rural South and into Northern and Midwestern cities.

1925 Tennessee tries John T. Scopes for teaching evolution in classroom.

1930 Twelve Southern intellectuals publish the agrarian manifesto *I'll Take My Stand*.

1933 F.D.R. unleashes the first wave of New Deal policies, which include the Tennessee Valley Act and the Agricultural Adjustment Act.

1934 Southern Tenant Farmer Union is founded.

1947 Committee of Racial Equality protests segregated seating on interstate buses in its "Journey of Reconciliation."

1948 South Carolina Governor Strom Thurmond and Mississippi Governor Fielding Wright run for President on a Dixiecrat ticket.

1954 Supreme Court declares segregation unconstitutional in *Brown v. Board of Education of Topeka, Kansas*.

1955 Rosa Parks is arrested for refusing to give up seat on a Montgomery, Alabama, bus. Bus boycott brings Martin Luther King, Jr., to national prominence.

1957 President Eisenhower sends troops to Little Rock, Arkansas, to enforce school integration. Southern Christian Leadership Conference forms.

1960 Civil right's protesters sit-in at Woolworth's in Greensboro, North Carolina.

1961 Freedom Riders protest over segregated buses in the lower South.

1963 Civil rights protests divide Birmingham, Alabama. Medgar Evers is murdered in Jackson, Mississippi. Over 250,000 Americans participate in March on Washington.

1964 Congress passes Civil Rights Act. Alabama Governor George Wallace urges disillusioned white Southerners to support Barry Goldwater's presidential bid. Senator Strom Thurmond changes his party allegiance and calls himself a "Goldwater Republican."

1965 Congress passes Voting Rights Act.

1967 Federal agents register black voters in sixty-two Southern counties.

1968 Martin Luther King, Jr., is assassinated. Nixon pursues successful Southern Strategy in Presidential election.

1970 Stone Mountain opens to the public.

1992 "Bubba Ticket" of Bill Clinton Al Gore win Presidency.

1996 Atlanta hosts the Summer Olympics.

Further Reading

Narrative Overviews and Reference Works

Boles, John B., *The South Through Time: A History of an American Region*, Prentice-Hall, 1995.

Cooper, William J., and Terrill, Thomas E., *The American South: A History*, McGraw Hill, 1991.

Hudson, Charles, *The Southeastern Indians*, University of Tennessee Press, 1976.

Roller, David C., and Twyman, Robert W., eds., *Encyclopedia of Southern History*, Louisiana State University Press, 1979.

Wilson, Charles Reagan, and Ferris, William, eds., *Encyclopedia of Southern Culture*, University of North Carolina Press, 1989.

Part I: The Nascent South

Berlin, Ira, *Many Thousands Gone: The First Two Centuries of Slavery in North America*, Belknap Press, 1998.

Klein, Rachel N., *The Unification of a Slave State: The Rise of the Planter Class in the South Carolina Backcountry, 1760–1808*, University of North Carolina Press, 1990.

Morgan, Edmund, *American Slavery / American Freedom*, W. W. Norton and Co., 1975.

Morgan, Philip D., *Slave Counterpoint: Black Culture in the Eighteenth-Century Chesapeake and Lowcountry*, University of North Carolina Press, 1997.

Usner, Daniel H., Jr., *Indians, Settlers, and Slaves in a Frontier Exchange Economy: The Lower Mississippi Valley Before 1783*, University of North Carolina Press, 1992.

Wood, Peter, *Black Majority: Negroes in Colonial South Carolina from 1670 through the Stono Rebellion*, New York: W. W. Norton and Co., 1974.

Part II: The Antebellum South

Fox-Genovese, Elizabeth, *Within the Plantation Household: Black and White Women of the Old South*, University of North Carolina Press, 1988.

Genovese, Eugene, *Roll, Jordan Roll: The World the Slaves Made*, Vintage Books, 1972.

Heyrman, Christine Leigh, *Southern Cross: The Beginnings of the Bible Belt*, University of North Carolina Press, 1997.

Potter, David M., *The Impending Crisis, 1848-1861*, Harper and Row, 1976.

Wright, L. Leitch, Jr., *The Only Land They Knew: The Tragic Story of the American Indians in the Old South*, University of Georgia Press, 1981.

Wyatt-Brown, Bertram, *Southern Honor: Ethics and Violence in the Old South*, Oxford University Press, 1982.

Part III: The Confederate South

Faust, Drew Gilpen, *Mothers of Invention: Women of the Slaveholding South in the American Civil War*, Vintage Press, 1996.

Foner, Eric, *Reconstruction: America's Unfinished Revolution, 1863–1877*, Harper and Row, 1988.

Gallagher, Gary W., *The Confederate War*, Harvard University Press, 1997.

McPherson, James M., *Battle Cry of Freedom: The Civil War Era*, Oxford University Press, 1988.

Thomas, Emory M., *The Confederate Nation, 1861–1865*, Harper Collins, 1979. *Robert E. Lee: A Biography*, W. W. Norton and Co., 1995.

Part IV: The New South

Ayers, Edward L., *The Promise of the New South: Life after Reconstruction*, Oxford University Press, 1992.

Cobb, James C., *The Most Southern Place on Earth: The Mississippi Delta and the Roots of Regional Identity*, Oxford University Press, 1992.

Doyle, Don H., *New Men, New Cities, New South: Atlanta, Nashville, Charleston, Mobile, 1860-1910*, University of North Carolina Press, 1990.

Foster, Gaines M., *Ghosts of the Confederacy: Defeat, The Lost Cause, and the Emergence of the New South, 1865–1913*, Oxford University Press, 1987.

Gaston, Paul, *The New South Creed*, Louisiana State University Press, 1970.

Woodward, C. Vann, *Origins of the New South*, Louisiana State University Press, 1951.

Part V: The Modern South

Bartley, Numan V., *The New South, 1945-1980*, Louisiana State University Press, 1995.

Carter, Dan T., *The Politics of Rage: George Wallace, the Origins of the New Conservatism, and the Transformation of American Politics*, Simon and Schuster, 1995.

Chafe, William H., *Civilities and Civil Rights: Greensboro, North Carolina, and the Black Struggle for Freedom*, Oxford University Press, 1981.

Dittmer, John, *Local People: The Struggle for Civil Rights in Mississippi*, University of Illinois Press, 1994.

Goldfield, David R., *Promised Land: The South Since 1945*, H. Davidson, Inc., 1987.

Grantham, Dewey W., *The South in Modern America: A Region at Odds*, Harper Collins, 1994.

Scher, Richard K., *Politics in the New South: Republicanism, Race and Leadership in the Twentieth Century*, M. E. Sharpe, 1997.

Index

MAP NAMES INDEX

Acknowledgments

Pictures are reproduced by permission of, or have been provided by the following:

Arcadia Editions Limited: 17
Betmann Archives: 116
British Library: 21
Hulton Getty: 59, 100
Library of Congress: 57
Map Collection, Yale University Library: 13
National Archives: 55, 66 (bottom), 67, 78, 80
National Gallery, London: 30
New York Historical Society: 49
North Carolina Division of Archives and History: 36
Olin Library, Cornell University: 26
Peter Newark American Pictures: 21, 120
Peter Newark Historical Pictures: 88
Private collections: 33, 34, 46, 68
Robert M. Hicklin, Jr., Spartanburg, South Carolina: 66 (top)
U.S. Army Military Historical Institute, Carlisle, Pennsylvania: 40l, 61
Philips Collection, Washington, D.C.: 103
SIPA-Press: 125
The Historic New Orleans Collection: 90
University of South Carolina, Columbia: 62
Werner Forman Archives: 15

Design and Cartography: Elsa Gibert and Malcolm Swanston (Arcadia Editions Limited).